FRANKLIN DELANO ROOSEVELT,

PRESIDENT

FRANKLIN DELANO
ROOSEVELT,
PRESIDENT

By John Devaney

Walker and Company
New York

First published in the United States of America in 1987 by the Walker Publishing Company, Inc.

Published simultaneously in Canada by John Wiley & Sons Canada, Limited, Rexdale, Ontario.

Book Design by Ellen Pugatch

Library of Congress Cataloging-in-Publication Data

Devaney, John.
    Franklin Delano Roosevelt, president.

    Includes index.
    Summary: A biography of the thirty-second President who, in four consecutive terms of office, led the country through the Depression and World War II.
    1. Roosevelt, Franklin D. (Franklin Delano), 1882-1945— Juvenile literature. 2. Presidents—United States—History—1933-1945—Juvenile literature. [1. Roosevelt, Franklin D. (Franklin Delano), 1882-1945. 2. Presidents] I. Title.
E807.D45   1987   973.917'092'4 [B] [92]   87-13808
ISBN 0-8027-6712-5
ISBN 8-8027-6713-3 (lib. bdg.)

Printed in the United States of America

10 9 8 7 6 5 4 3 2 1

To Barbara

All photographs courtesy of the Franklin D. Roosevelt Library.

Please note that some of these photographs are not of the quality that the publisher would wish, due to the photographic techniques of that period. However, they have been included in this book for their historical significance.

Contents

ACKNOWLEDGMENTS

Both during and after Franklin's lifetime, hundreds of books were written about the nation's only four-term president. Of those hundreds, I have read almost a dozen. I would recommend these to readers who want to know more about Franklin and Eleanor.

FDR: An Intimate History, by Nathan Miller; *Roosevelt in Retrospect,* by John Gunther; *The Man Who . . . ,* by Richard Oulahan; *Eleanor and Franklin,* by Joseph Lash; *The Beckoning of History,* by Kenneth S. Davis; *Road to the White House,* by Lorena Hickock; *Roosevelt: An Informal Biography,* by Alden Hatch; and *Roosevelt, The Lion and the Fox,* by James McGregor Burns.

For those who want to delve more deeply into the life of Franklin and the rest of the Roosevelts, a trip to Hyde Park, New York, and the Franklin D. Roosevelt Library will be full of revelations. The library— and the mansion in which Franklin was born and grew up—is open to the public for a nominal fee.—J.D.

Franklin Delano Roosevelt radiates his charming smile as he prepares to speak on the radio with the vibrant voice that thrilled millions. He taught future presidents and other politicians how to speak in an easy conversational style on the radio. Up to then, politicians had roared on the radio the way they roared on platforms. Many of Franklin's speeches were known as "fireside chats."

1

A Strange Wish

The President of the United States sat at his desk in the White House. Beads of sweat glistened on his whiskered face. He stared out through a window to see horse-drawn carriages trot slowly through Washington's sticky heat. This was the hottest day of the summer of 1887.

An aide told the President that the man from New York waited to see him in the Green Room. President Grover Cleveland nodded. He hoped the New York man would accept his offer to become ambassador to The Netherlands. That would be one problem solved.

The President sighed as he walked to the Green Room. So many problems nagged at him. New labor unions insisted on higher wages. Farmers cried out for higher prices. Businessmen growled that he was a Democrat who couldn't be trusted.

"It is good of you to come to see me," President Cleveland said as he greeted the tall New Yorker. At the man's knee stood a small boy. "My son, Franklin," the visitor said to the President.

"Franklin," the President said, "I am very glad to make your acquaintance." The President shook Franklin's little hand.

"Thank you very much, Mr. President," the five-year-old boy said. He had repeated what his father had told him to say.

The men sat down. Franklin sat in a chair with his legs dangling. The New Yorker told President Cleveland that he had to say no to the offer to be ambassador. He didn't want to move his wife and son away from their rambling farm high above the Hudson River.

1

An infant Franklin rides the shoulder of his father.

The President frowned—another problem still unresolved. He arose and put his hand atop Franklin's head.

"Little man," the President said, "I am making a strange wish for you. It is that you may never be President of the United States."

Franklin Delano Roosevelt stared upward at the President, too startled to speak.

2

"A Born Sailor, a True Delano"

"Let's play horsey!" Four-year-old Franklin, his blue eyes flashing, wanted to play a game with his two-year-old cousin Eleanor. The bashful Eleanor stared at the floor.

"Go with Franklin, Granny," said Eleanor's mother, who was visiting Franklin's parents. She called Eleanor "Granny" because, she said, the little girl "acted like an old lady."

Eleanor Roosevelt trailed her cousin Franklin up the stairs of his parents' 35-room mansion. The two children scampered into Franklin's room.

Franklin told Eleanor to climb onto his back to play horsey. "You say, 'Giddyap,' " he shouted.

"Giddyap!" Eleanor shrilled. She was scared. She hated games.

Franklin banged across the floor on all fours. Eleanor shrieked. She grabbed Franklin's neck with a choking grip. He screamed.

Their parents heard the bangs and shrieks. They ran up the stairs.

"Granny! Let go of Franklin!" her mother snapped. Franklin's father, James Roosevelt, turned to Eleanor's mother, and said, laughing, "Your daughter seems to have made a conquest!"

Claes Martenszen van Rosenvelt came to America from The Netherlands in 1636. He tilled a farm in what is now the Harlem area of Manhattan and became prosperous. Over the next century,

3

Franklin rides on one of the mules on the Roosevelt estate at Hyde Park. Also aboard is one of many dogs his father gave him. His mother, like many mothers of the time, dressed the boy in skirts. When he was about 6, he rebelled, insisting on his first trousers.

as Dutch-owned New Amsterdam became English-owned New York, the van Rosenvelts became the Roosevelts.

By 1880 there were two branches of the New York Roosevelts. One branch lived on Long Island and was known as the Oyster Bay Roosevelts. The other branch lived near the village of Hyde Park on the Hudson River, about a hundred miles north of Manhattan. This branch was known as the Hudson River Roosevelts.

James Roosevelt was the vice president of a company that owned railroad, coal and other huge enterprises. Monopolies, or trusts as they were called, were then legal. The trusts choked off competitors and boosted prices to whatever levels the trusts wanted. The wealthy James bought hundreds of acres of farmland along the Hudson, near Poughkeepsie, where he had grown up. He liked to roam the estate, which he called Springwood. It was about a mile south of Hyde Park. Riding on horseback in expensive clothes, the country squire oversaw his crops and cattle.

James' first wife had died. In the spring of 1880 he went to a party at the Manhattan home of an Oyster Bay cousin, Mrs. Theodore Roosevelt. Her son, whom everyone called Teddy, attended Harvard. Teddy talked about going into politics. The Roosevelts were esteemed members of Manhattan society's elite "400." The "400" were the oldest and among the wealthiest families in Manhattan. The "400" looked down their noses at politics—the begging of votes from the lower classes. "Politics," James told his friends, "is a dirty business."

At the party a tall and stately beauty, Sara Delano, entranced James. As a teenager she had sailed across the Pacific to China on a tall ship with her father, Warren Delano, a skipper and trader. He had become a millionaire. At parties, Sallie, as her friends called her, sang the sea chanteys of her girlhood:

Down the river hailed a Yankee clipper,
And it's blow, my bully boys, blow!

Sara, better known to her friends as Sallie, poses with her only child. For this portrait, she dressed him in a Scottish boy's kilt. Sara adored her father, Warren Delano, and often said that the only man she would have married was James, who was almost twice her age.

In this faded photo from the family album, Franklin (left) grips the wheel of the family's boat, the *Half Moon*, as it glides across the Bay of Fundy. Some ten years later, when Franklin was 16, he sailed a boat all by himself from New York to Maine.

In the fall of 1880 she and James married. Their first—and only—child was born on January 30, 1882, in the Hyde Park mansion. A proud father wrote in his diary: "At quarter to nine my Sallie had a splendid large baby boy. He weighs 10 pounds without clothes." His parents named him Franklin Delano.

The splendid baby grew into a small but wiry boy. His father, now over 50 and old enough to be his grandfather, gave him all a boy could want. Franklin had a dog when he was two, a pony when he was four, a rifle when he was ten.

He tramped through the woods with his father, who taught him how to tell a maple from an oak. Together they flew on an ice boat, sails billowing, across the frozen Hudson. They rode on horseback as James showed Franklin how to watch for a sick cow and when to plant a crop of corn.

In the summers the family went to Campobello, an island off the coast of Maine. James owned a huge house on Campobello. Franklin stood with his father on the pitching deck of the family's 51-foot schooner, the *Half Moon*. James gripped the wheel to show Franklin how to steer the *Half Moon* through the tricky currents in the Bay of Fundy. "He's a born sailor," his mother told friends, "a true Delano!"

The outdoor life seemed to harden the boy, who came only to the shoulders of most boys his age. One day a friend swung a stick that accidently struck Franklin across the mouth. Blood gushed from his mouth, and air cut like a knife into a dangling nerve.

Franklin stumbled home, doubled over, cupping his bleeding mouth with his hand. His mother saw him washing off the blood. She took him to a dentist who closed the wound and capped his teeth.

His mother scolded him for trying to hide the injury. But it was clear her son, the grandson of a tough sea captain, was indeed a true Delano.

Later a friend asked Franklin why he had tried to hide the injury from his parents. Franklin knew his father had become sickly. "They were always considerate to me," he said. "I didn't want them to worry."

3

"By Wingo! They Nearly Starved!"

Franklin did not go to a school. No country school could possibly be good enough for the Roosevelts' only child. Sara hired tutors to teach him at home. One of those tutors was a young French woman, Jeanne Sandoz. She taught Franklin how to speak and write French. She read to him the plays of Shakespeare. She taught history to him.

One day she talked to him about the plight of people crushed under the heels of cruel rulers. She asked Franklin to write a report on how ancient Egyptian kings brutalized their people.

Franklin wrote: "The working people had nothing. The kings made them work so hard and gave them so little that by wingo! they nearly starved and by jinks! they had hardly any clothes so they died in the quadrillions."

Living on his rich father's estate, Franklin did not know that a hundred miles to the south, men, women and children starved in icy cold tenements of New York City's slums.

His father tried to help the poor. He volunteered to raise money for the Hyde Park hospital and the village's home for the poor and aged. But James would have said a loud "no" to anyone who suggested that the government give taxpayers' money to the poor.

James believed in *noblesse oblige*, what the French call the aristocrat's duty to be fatherly to the peasant. James thought the rich—not the government—owed a duty to the poor.

9

Both of Franklin's parents joined in his education. Franklin's mother, the sea captain's daughter, read stories to him before he could read. When he learned to read, he sat for hours over books about sea battles. At 12 he had read all the books on sea power by Captain Alfred Mahan, whose books were also being read by the admirals of the world's naval powers: England, Germany and Japan.

As a girl in China, Sara had collected stamps of foreign countries. She gave Franklin her collection. She told him that stamps told much of a nation's history and culture. Franklin began to add to the collection by stripping stamps from mail his father received from foreign countries. He used a magnifying glass to peer at the stamps and place them in his stamp books.

There were only a few boys his age to play with on an estate a mile from the nearest village. One day he and a friend started to argue. They threw fists at each other.

Franklin's father stopped them. Later he said to Franklin, "There is an old saying, 'The one who can't think of a good argument is the one who strikes the first blow.' "

When he played with other boys, Franklin shouted orders. His mother suggested that sometimes he let the others give orders.

"Mummy," he said, "if I didn't give the orders, nothing would happen."

Franklin's favorite place at Hyde Park was the family library. Books stood floor to ceiling. He read the books shelf by shelf. When magazines came to Hyde Park from overseas, Franklin ran off with them. "And what he reads," a proud Sara told friends, "he seems to remember with a memory that's like flypaper—everything sticks to it."

She had reason to know his memory was excellent. One day she read to him while he studied his books of stamps. She thought he was not listening to her. "I don't think there is any point in reading to you anymore," she said. She slapped shut the book.

"Why?" he asked. Then he recited word for word the last paragraph she had read. "Mama," he told her, "I would be ashamed of myself if I couldn't do at least two things at once."

Franklin stands behind one of the tripod-mounted cameras his father gave him. He is wearing the knickers that were popular then among teenage boys. His hobbies included photography, stamp collecting, bird study and forestry. He kept up with those interests all of his life.

He seemed eager to cast out a net and gather in as many things as possible to study and master. He walked alone in the woods and studied the trees. At 14 he knew as much about forestry as his father.

When his father gave him a rifle to shoot birds, it was on one condition. Franklin was to shoot only one bird in a species. Each bird he shot was stuffed. At 15 he owned one of the best bird collections in the Hudson Valley.

His father gave him a camera. Franklin took the camera apart and studied how each part worked. When he took pictures, he developed the film himself in a basement dark room.

One rainy afternoon, when he was 14, his mother came into his room. He was turning the pages of a dictionary.

"There are a lot of words I don't understand," he told her. "I started reading the dictionary page by page and I'm almost halfway through."

Nearly every summer he and his parents traveled to Europe aboard a steamship. When Franklin was 14, he and his tutor, a young man in his 20s, bought bicycles and sped off together on a tour of Germany. His parents told him to meet them in Belgium.

One evening Franklin and the tutor sped into a German town at dusk. Their bikes bounced along the cobbled streets.

"Halt!" a voice cried out in German.

Franklin and the tutor saw a row of helmeted soldiers facing them. The soldiers gripped rifles with bayonets poking from the muzzles. The tutor braked his bike so suddenly that he fell off the bike.

A soldier lunged forward, thrusting his bayonet at the young man's throat.

Franklin jumped off his bike and ran toward the tutor and the gleaming bayonet.

4

"Let's Run Away and Join the Navy!"

"They sure have a lot of laws in Germany," Franklin said to his father. "One law says you can't enter a German city on a bike after dark."

"Did the soldiers hurt you, Franklin?" his mother asked.

Franklin had just arrived in a Belgian city to join his parents. He told them how the soldiers had stopped him and his tutor. "An officer," he said, "told us to go outside the city and come back on a train, the legal way to enter the city."

Franklin thought that his adventure would be a thrilling one to tell the new friends he would make at Groton. Now 14, Franklin entered Groton in the fall of 1896. Located near Boston, Groton was a school for society's "400." Groton trained boys to become leaders in business.

The 14-year-old Franklin stood five-foot-one and weighed about 100 pounds. He had to look up at the boys he met during the first days at Groton. The other boys in his class had attended Groton for the past two years. They laughed at the new boy because, they said, "you talk funny." Franklin had picked up a British accent during his visits to Europe.

He copied the way the other "Grotties" spoke. He stretched out his words so that a one-syllable word like "my" became two syllables: "My-ah." It was a way of speaking—as though he had marbles in his mouth," some people said—that would entrance Americans 40 years later.

Franklin crouches with another one of the family dogs that romped at Hyde Park. Now about 15, the once-small and wiry boy was stretching into a willowy teenager.

Life at Groton was gruelling. When Franklin arrived, he had to stand against a wall while boys hit his ankles with hockey sticks. If he cried, he was a panty-waist. He did not cry.

The boys awoke at seven. They took cold showers even on icy winter days. They marched to breakfast and to morning chapel.

The school's headmaster, an Episcopal minister, read prayers. They attended classes—Greek, French, algebra, literature, sacred studies—until three, stopping only at noon for the main meal of the day.

At three the boys charged out onto playing fields. Every Grottie had to play football in the fall and winter, baseball in the spring. If a boy didn't, he had no "school spirit"—and that could mean a beating from the other boys.

Little Franklin stood in the line for the school's worst football team. Six-foot fullbacks rammed over him. Each evening he limped back to his bare-walled cell. It had no door, only a curtain. He washed his bruised face in a sink. He ate a light supper, attended chapel and studied alone.

At ten o'clock the boys walked in a line to the cottage of the headmaster. Each boy shook the headmaster's hand and wished him good night.

A pampered boy had plunged into a world as strict and bare as military barracks. He told his parents that he was happy. When Groton won a big football game, he wrote to his mother: "I am hoarse, deaf and ready to stand on my cocoanut."

He revered the headmaster, the Reverend Endicott Peabody. He listened as Peabody told the boys to follow the example of Franklin's cousin, Teddy Roosevelt. A Republican, Teddy had been elected to the New York State legislature. Now, with a Republican in the White House, he had been appointed assistant secretary of the navy.

Rich young men should follow Teddy into politics, Peabody told Grotties. "If the better people don't run for office," he told them, "this nation will be ruled by ruffians."

Franklin envied his cousin Teddy. Imagine being the No. 2 boss of the navy. The No. 2 boss could stand on the bridge of a battleship and maybe even steer it as the dreadnaught pounded through the ocean with its guns poking above the horizon. Franklin knew now what he wanted to be after Groton: a naval officer. One day he would command a battleship.

Suddenly, in the fall of 1898, he saw a chance to ride into battle on a warship. The U.S. battleship *Maine* blew up in a Cuban harbor. Congress declared war on Spain, which owned Cuba. American soldiers and sailors sailed to Cuba, shouting, "Remember the *Maine!*"

Teddy Roosevelt banded together a bunch of cowboys from the west. He called them his "Rough Riders." Colonel Roosevelt and his Rough Riders splashed ashore in Cuba as the spearhead of the invading American army.

Franklin rode with them in his imagination. One day he said to a friend, "Let's run away from school and join the navy."

"We're too young. You have to be eighteen."

"We'll fake our names. We look eighteen."

The scrawny Franklin did not look eighteen. But he talked a delivery man into hiding him and his friend on a wagon when it left school the next day. But that night both boys felt feverish. The next morning both tossed on a hospital bed, ill with scarlet fever.

Sara and her husband, who was by now almost an invalid, came home from Europe as fast as they could travel. Sara left her husband at Hyde Park and rushed to Groton. She worried about Franklin. Germs seemed to strike him down more often than they hit other boys. All his life, Franklin had been bedded by colds, fevers, sore throats, earaches. But he always bounced back. After several weeks in bed, he recovered from the scarlet fever.

Franklin read newspapers that told of Cousin Teddy's daring in Cuba. Teddy led his Rough Riders up San Juan Hill and gunned down Spanish defenders. Teddy's charge avenged the sinking of the *Maine*. The war was won, and Teddy came home a hero. That fall of 1898 he ran for governor of New York and won with an avalanche of votes.

Each Christmas Franklin came home to Hyde Park. All the Roosevelts gathered for a huge party. The prettiest of the girls was Alice Roosevelt, Teddy's daughter. Franklin and Alice danced together up and down the room, her blue eyes sparkling as the dancers sang, "Ta-ra-ra-*boom*-de-ay . . ."

The dance ended. Franklin mopped his brow. He saw a tall,

gawky girl with prominent front teeth standing alone in a corner. She looked sad, almost ready to cry.

It was Eleanor, the cousin who had tried to ride on his back.

Franklin walked to her side. She looked surprised. No boy had talked to her yet.

"Eleanor, will you have this next dance with me?"

Eleanor's face lit with a sunny radiance. For an instant, Franklin thought, she was the most beautiful girl in the room.

"Oh, Franklin," she said, "I'd love to."

5

"Oh Fear to Call It Loving"

Franklin and his father sat before a fireplace in the Hyde Park mansion. A shawl covered his father's thin shoulders. The fire's light flickered on his pale, drawn face. Now 71, weakened by an ailing heart, James Roosevelt was dying.

On this fall day in 1899, Franklin had come home from Groton to tell his father that he wanted to go to Annapolis and become a navy officer. Gently, his father reminded him: One day, perhaps soon, Franklin would be the master of this house and the Roosevelt fortune. How could he watch over the estate and care for his mother if he were a thousand miles at sea?

Franklin nodded slowly. He was now 17. The three years at Groton had changed a small, wiry boy into a willowy 5-foot-9, 130-pound teenager.

Franklin stared for several minutes at the fire. In the rising gray smoke he saw vanishing dreams—the dreams of guns thundering.

He turned to his father, the father who had always given him everything he asked. Franklin smiled weakly, but in a strong voice he said, "All right, papa, Harvard it is."

At Harvard he lived in an area of Boston called The Gold Coast. Only the wealthiest students could pay for the expensive rooms. Like other society gentlemen, Franklin did not study too hard. He got what were called "a gentleman's Cs."

He needed to wear glasses. He chose a style called pince-nez that clipped onto the bridge of the nose. To see people better, he

18

tossed back his head as he faced them. Taller than most, he had to look down. The tossing of the head, the glance downward—a manner he would keep all his life—made people think he stared down his nose at them with contempt.

Harvard men called him snooty. When he applied to join the best social club at Harvard, the members rejected him. Later he called the snub "the worst disappointment of my life." Harvard men said the snub gave him an inferiority complex which he tried to mask, they said, by acting in a cocky, arrogant way.

Even his friends at Groton and Harvard said he had "an independent, cocky manner, a person who was very argumentative and sarcastic." Girls called him a "feather duster," meaning that behind the snooty, knowing manner sat a lightweight brain. Years later, political foes would also see nothing in Franklin, a blindness that would cost them dearly.

At Groton he had yearned to win cheers and his mother's applause by being a football or baseball hero. But as he conceded, he was a "B.B.B.B.—a Bum Base Ball Batter." His mother boasted to friends that he won the job of the manager of the Groton baseball team. But that only meant he had to bring the bats and balls to the games. He knew the job was no great honor, but he let his mother think it was.

At Harvard he set a goal—one that his mother would be proud of if he reached it. He wanted to be editor of the university's daily paper, The Harvard *Crimson*. He went to work as a reporter. One day he rushed up to the editor and shouted, "I have a scoop! The vice president of the United States will speak tomorrow at Harvard!" Like all Harvard boys, he pronounced the name as "Hahvahd."

The *Crimson* editor bannered the story across the front page. The vice president was the stocky, walrus-mustached Teddy Roosevelt. In 1900, the Republicans had picked him as vice president, William McKinley as President. The McKinley-Roosevelt ticket won. Knowing that Teddy had arrived in Boston, Franklin phoned him. Teddy told him he was coming to Harvard to speak to a

The B.B.B.B.—Bum Base Ball Batter—wears one of the straw "boaters"
of the time as he stands for a team photograph with the Groton baseball
team. As manager, he selected three other students as comanagers. They
shared the work while he made three friends grateful—one of the first
of a lifetime of shrewd political moves.

government class. Franklin's scoop made the other reporters jealous. Franklin had taken a big step toward sitting in the editor's chair.

Just after Franklin entered Harvard in the fall of 1900, his father died. The next summer, 1901, he finished his freshman year and sailed with his mother to Europe. In Paris they read that a gunman had shot President McKinley. When they got off the boat in New York, they learned that McKinley had died of his wounds. Cousin Teddy had become the President of the United States.

"That cowboy in the White House," as wealthy men began to call Teddy, campaigned for laws to break up the trusts, the monopolies that had made men like the Rockefellers, Astors, Mellons—and James Roosevelt—rich. Teddy called himself a Progressive. He set out to raise wages and lower working hours, especially for women and children laboring in factories. Members of society's "400" called the Oyster Bay Roosevelt "a traitor to his class."

Teddy's daughter, the pretty Alice, became the idol of young people. They called her Princess Alice. With shining, envious eyes, they read in newspapers about her glittering parties in the White House. Alice often invited her cousin, Franklin, to dance the night away at those parties. Alice's cousin, Eleanor, came from New York. She sometimes slept over and had breakfast the next morning with her uncle, the President.

Eleanor's father was Teddy's brother, Elliot Roosevelt. Elliot often staggered home drunk. He and Eleanor's mother quarreled about his drinking. When Eleanor was nine, her father left home. A year later, in 1893, her mother died during a diptheria epidemic.

Eleanor lived with her rich grandmother in a Manhattan townhouse. One day her father came by to take her for a walk. She adored him. He called her "Little Nell." He stopped at a bar and left Eleanor in a cloakroom. She sat there for six hours. She saw her father carried out drunk, heels first. A doorman took her home.

A year later Elliot died. At 12 Eleanor was an orphan.

Her strict grandmother kept her in little girls' short gowns even though she was tall. At parties other girls snickered when she came by. Eleanor's aunts called her "the ugly duckling."

Eleanor attended a school for girls in England that was similar to Groton. It was Eleanor's dream to go to college, but her grandmother said no. Eleanor took a job as an unpaid social worker. The niece of the President of the United States visited cold tenements to give food and medicine to sick mothers and scrawny children, the families of workers who made one dollar a day.

Franklin met Eleanor at White House parties. Unknown to his mother, who kept a wary eye on girls who talked to her only son, Franklin began to come to New York from Harvard to see Eleanor. She took him to tenements where he saw rats scurry near the cribs of babies. Leaving a smelly tenement one evening, he said to her, "I never had any idea that anybody had to live that way."

One weekend in the fall of 1903, now the *Crimson* editor, he asked Eleanor to come to Harvard for a football game. After the game they went to Groton. They strolled along a river bank. Couples rode by on horse-drawn carriages, the women in long gowns and wide hats, the men in high starched collars and derbies or straw "boaters."

As they strolled, Franklin turned to Eleanor and asked her to marry him. She wasn't surprised, even though they had been "courting," as people said then, only a few months. She knew a lot about him. She knew that he yearned to be successful, maybe even as famous as Teddy. He knew that she wanted a happy, loving family life—a life she had never known.

She did not say yes or no. Two days later she wrote to him and quoted lines from a poem: "Unless you can swear for life, for death/ Oh fear to call it loving."

Franklin wrote back. He swore his love for life and until death. Eleanor said yes.

A startled Sara was appalled. How could he marry a girl whom Sara called, with pity in her voice, "poor sweet Eleanor?" The family's ugly duckling. She wondered how her handsome son, now

The editor of The Harvard *Crimson* sits with fellow board members. Franklin took enough courses at Groton to get him through Harvard in only three years. He could have graduated in 1903. But he took extra courses in the 1903–1904 school year so he could be the *Crimson* editor. He got his diploma with the class of 1904, and always called himself a member of that '04 class.

six feet tall with the athletic body and sun-bronzed face of a sea captain, could have picked Eleanor. But others wondered what the wealthy niece of the nation's President saw in Franklin.

Eleanor tried to win over Sara. She wrote a meek note: "Dear Cousin Sallie, It is impossible to tell you how I feel toward Franklin. I can only say that my one great wish is always to prove worthy of him . . . I do want you to love me a little. You must know that I will always try to do as you wish . . ."

Sara tried to delay the marriage. She worried that the couple was too young, and hoped that Franklin would find someone else. Franklin made an end run around his mother. This was a tactic he would use often against her and, later, in politics against his foes. He never argued with her about his choice of Eleanor. He simply slipped off to make his own plans. Suddenly, one day, Sara learned the wedding date had been set—March 17, 1905.

A huge crowd milled around the Manhattan townhouse where Eleanor and Franklin were to be married. Men and women gaped as ornate carriages pulled up to the curb. Ladies stepped out holding the skirts of their brocaded gowns, necks and wrists glittering with silver and gold jewelry. Gentlemen strode into the house wearing top hats and tails.

"Look at the swells!" the spectators exclaimed, enviously watching society's rich "400."

A row of dirty-faced boys from a nearby slum sat atop a high fence so they could see that era's beautiful people. A large carriage, pulled by two white horses, turned off Fifth Avenue and rolled down the street. "Here he comes!" one boy shouted. "Hooray for Teddy!" piped up several others.

The President of the United States turned toward the boys. The President pretended to be angry at the shouting boys. He wiggled a finger at the boys in a scolding way. Then, suddenly, he flashed a smile that told the cheering boys that they were his kind of people.

6

The Way to the
White House

A nervous Eleanor stood tall and slender. She wore a lacey white wedding dress that swirled at the floor and trailed behind her. She gripped the arm of her uncle, the President of the United States. She and Teddy walked to the center of the room. The Reverend Endicott Peabody, the headmaster from Groton, waited with his prayer book in hand.

Franklin stepped forward. The President gave his niece to the tall groom. Reverend Peabody read the prayers of the wedding ceremony. He pronounced Franklin and Eleanor husband and wife. The guests surged forward to encircle the newlyweds and wish them well.

Teddy shook Franklin's hand. "There's nothing like keeping the name in the family," he said in his booming voice. He walked into the next room where servants waited with trays of food and drinks. The guests followed after him.

Franklin and Eleanor stood alone, suddenly forgotten. The spotlight of attention was on the President. Presidents, Eleanor and Franklin had just learned, have a way of taking the spotlight with them.

Franklin and Eleanor moved into a Manhattan townhouse bought for them by Franklin's mother, who had inherited millions from her husband and her father. At Harvard, Franklin had reached his goal—he became the editor of the *Crimson*. But he did not want

25

Eleanor sits in a gondola in Venice, holding a paper and Franklin's straw "boater." Franklin took this photo during the newlyweds' honeymoon trip to Europe in the spring of 1905. They also visited England, France and Switzerland, where Franklin climbed a mountain.

to be a newspaperman. He studied law at Columbia, passed the exams to be a lawyer and went to work as a lawyer in the big-money world of Wall Street. A year after their marriage, Eleanor gave birth to their first child, Anna.

One late afternoon in the fall of 1907, Franklin sat with several other lawyers as they chatted about their ambitions. "I don't intend to practice law forever," Franklin said. "I will run for office the first chance I get—the way Teddy did. First, I will win a seat in the state legislature. I will become assistant secretary of the navy. Then I will be governor of New York. And anyone who is governor of New York has a good chance to be President with any luck."

The lawyers did not laugh at Franklin's prediction. They knew that the steps in the path Franklin had just traced—from state legislator to assistant secretary of the navy to governor to President—were the same steps made by the man who now sat in the White House, Franklin's cousin Teddy.

In Washington Teddy pounded his huge fist on the desk and demanded that Congress pass his Progressive laws. Teddy wanted to break up the trusts that kept prices high and wages low. He wanted to lower the working hours of women and children in factories. One day Franklin and Eleanor visited him in the White House. Teddy paced in front of a fireplace and roared, "If I could be Congress for just ten minutes, I would pass all the laws I need to make this country better for the working man and woman!"

In 1909 Teddy left the White House, his second term ended. A fellow Republican, William Howard Taft, won the Presidency. He promised to work for Progressive laws. Teddy went to Africa to hunt lions. A rich man on Wall Street said to a friend, "I hope the lions will do their duty."

The Roosevelt name was still a magic one to most Americans. In 1910 a group of Hyde Park Democrats asked Franklin to run for the New York State Senate. Franklin knew that Republicans had won that Senate seat for almost 50 years. But this was the chance at politics that he had been seeking. He said yes.

Franklin hired a flashy red roadster. He drove it over bumpy back roads to speak to farmers and people in small villages. He began his speeches by drawing out the words in his caramel-rich voice, "Myyyy--ahhhh frrr-iendssss . . ." He made people believe he really was their friend. He told them how he would fight for ways to get higher prices for their crops. He promised laws that would stop big city businessmen from cheating the farmer when crops came to city markets.

Franklin won. Republicans were shocked. Early in 1911 he moved with his family from Manhattan to New York's capital in Albany. By now he and Eleanor had three children: Anna, 5, James, 3, and Elliot, who had been born the previous September. Hours after he stepped off the train in Albany, Franklin plunged into what he loved all his life—a political scrap.

At that time, state legislators picked the two U.S. senators from each state. (In 1913 an amendment to the Constitution allowed voters to pick their senators.) The potbellied, balding William "Boss" Murphy, a cigar sticking out of his mouth, ruled the Tammany Tigers. Tammany, a political powerhouse, got votes for its candidates by giving money, food and jobs to voters. Tammany candidates nearly always won in New York City. But to be a Tammany candidate, a politician had to do what Boss Murphy told him to do. (There were no women candidates because women then were not allowed to vote.)

Boss Murphy told the state legislators to pick his crony, "Blue-Eyed Billy" Sheehan, as U.S. senator.

"No, sir!" Franklin snapped at Boss Murphy. Franklin told other legislators that Blue-Eyed Billy would be good for Tammany and its crooked politicians—but bad for the people.

Legislators joined Franklin in the mansion he had rented in Albany. The rebels refused to sit in the State senate. The state senate could pass no laws. The state's machinery clanked to a stop. For ten weeks it remained stopped. Boss Murphy pleaded and threatened. He scared some senators. They wanted to surrender. But at Franklin's side, whispering in his ear, stood a man with a thin, pock-marked face. He called himself "the ugliest man in the world." Louis Howe wrote about politics for newspapers. He knew ways to beat bosses like Murphy. He gave advice to Franklin: "hang on, don't quit, he will have to surrender."

Howe liked the handsome, rich Franklin with the vote-getting last name. Howe told reporters, "This Roosevelt could be a fast-rising, shooting star like his cousin Teddy."

Boss Murphy had to give in. He named another Tammany man to be senator. "I can vote for him," Franklin said. "He's not a 'yes man' who will do everything Murphy says."

The rebels went back to their seats. New York State began to run again. Newspapers hailed Franklin as a hero, a knight who had jousted with a big city boss, and won.

Politicians across the nation had followed Franklin's fight blow by blow. In nearby New Jersey, a thin, bespectacled former college professor, Woodrow Wilson, had been elected governor. A Democrat, he stood for the ideals of Progressivism. He scorned city bosses. "That young man Roosevelt," Governor Wilson said to an aide, "will bear watching."

Franklin tossed in his bed, his face beaded with sweat. Eleanor watched over with concern.

"I feel awful, Babs," he said. Babs, for baby, was his favorite name for her. "The election is only two months away, and I can't get out of bed to campaign."

He thought for several moments, then looked up at Eleanor and said quickly, "Send for Louis Howe!"

In the summer of 1912 Franklin and "the three chicks," as he called his children, had gone to Campobello. He sailed on the Bay of Fundy at the wheel of his new boat, the *Full Moon*. His three children sat on the deck and watched with awe as the bronzed 6-foot, 190-pound giant jockeyed the pitching boat through high waves.

Suddenly, the giant was felled by another one of those germs that struck him down so often. This time it was typhoid fever. He had to run for reelection to the Senate. He could not make a speech—he could not even climb out of bed—because he felt so ill and weary.

Louis Howe knew how to get votes. He came to Manhattan, where Franklin lay ill. He agreed to run Franklin's campaign for $100 a week. It would be a campaign in which the candidate could not be seen nor heard.

Howe mailed out thousands of letters and pamphlets that praised Franklin. Howe said that Franklin stood with Woodrow Wilson, who had been nominated by the Democrats to run for President. Wilson and Franklin, wrote Howe, wanted higher taxes on the rich, better pay for the laborer and higher prices for the farmer. They favored Progressive laws which tried to make life easier for women and children toiling 12 hours a day in sweatshop factories.

The Republicans again picked William Howard Taft. Teddy Roosevelt growled that Taft had caved in to the monopolies of millionaires like John D. Rockefeller. Teddy decided to run for the presidency as a third-party Progressive. He became the first to try to be President for three terms.

Franklin had to watch the 1912 presidential campaigns—and his own—from a bed. On election night, pale and thin, he gripped the phone as Louis Howe called in the results. Franklin's smile grew wide. He had won. An hour later he learned that the nation's new President was a fellow Democrat—Woodrow Wilson.

Eleanor had not liked the dirty-looking Howe whose cigarettes dangled from his lips. Now she stared at him, stunned. He had won the election for her husband even though the candidate could not speak to the voters. She wondered how he had done it.

The political education of another Roosevelt had begun.

Eleanor and Franklin went to Washington early in 1913 to watch Wilson's inauguration. On a street Franklin met Josephus Daniels, a North Carolina newspaper editor. Wilson had picked Daniels, a Progressive Democrat, as his secretary of the navy.

Daniels knew that Wilson liked Franklin. And Daniels knew that Franklin, a sailor since boyhood, knew more about navies and sea power than he, a landlubber, would ever know.

"How," asked Daniels, "would you like to come to Washington as my assistant secretary of the navy?"

"I would like it bully well!" Franklin exploded, surprise all over his face. Only six years earlier he had said that the No. 2 navy job was the second step toward the presidency after the state legislature—and now the job was being offered to him on a platter!

A few weeks later Daniels and Franklin posed for a photo on a balcony of the navy's building near the White House. Daniels saw a huge grin on Franklin's face.

"I will tell you why you are smiling," Daniels said with a little laugh. "We are both looking down at the White House and you are saying to yourself, 'Someday I will be living in that house.' "

Franklin tossed back his head and laughed. But he did not say that Daniels was wrong.

7

"We Have to Go to War!"

President Wilson rubbed a thin hand across his pointed chin as he scanned the paper on his desk. Franklin stood at his side in the White House on a warm spring day in 1916. The White House had become a familiar place to the 34-year-old Franklin. He had first visited it as a boy almost 30 years earlier. Ten years ago he had come here often to see his cousin Teddy, the President. Now, as assistant secretary of the navy, he came often to report to President Wilson on how he and Josephus Daniels were building the United States Navy into a world seapower.

Guns roared across Europe. British and French armies battled German and Austrian troops on muddy, cratered battlefields. Millions of men had been killed. Exhausted soldiers cowered in trenches, deadly shrapnel from exploding shells rained down around them. Neither side could advance.

In England and Germany, women and children waited in long lines for a loaf of stale bread. German subs torpedoed ships carrying food and supplies to England. British warships fought back and tried to sink German boats.

Then German subs torpedoed American ships. President Wilson warned the Germans: these U-boat attacks could draw the United States into the war against Germany.

In 1914, when the war began, Europeans had laughed at the U.S. Navy as "a bathtub fleet." They laughed no more. Daniels and Franklin had begged Congress for money to build battleships, cruisers, destroyers and ships to carry those new airplanes—ships called aircraft carriers. Soon, Franklin told the President, the United States would have a "two-ocean fleet," one that could battle Japan, a rising power, in the Pacific, and blow up German U-boats in the Atlantic.

As President Wilson read Franklin's latest report, Franklin asked him for permission to order the navy's Atlantic fleet into action against the German subs. Cousin Teddy had told Franklin only a few days earlier: "We have to get into this war to stop Germany from taking over Europe!" Franklin agreed with Teddy.

The President looked at Franklin angrily. "No!" the President snapped.

Franklin's face flushed. He walked stiffly toward the door.

"Wait!" the President commanded.

Franklin turned. "I owe you an explanation," the President said slowly. He told Franklin that he wanted history books to show "that war had been forced on us deliberately by Germany." He did not want history to say that Americans jumped across the Atlantic to pick a fight with Germany.

Some 25 years later, Franklin told friends how Wilson had agonized over going to war. Franklin—those 25 years later—had to go through the same agony.

Franklin rode on navy ships whenever he could get away from Washington. He had dreamed of being an admiral. Now, the boss of admirals, he marched up ship gangways as guns roared him a 17-gun salute. Franklin stood on the bridge of battleships as the dreadnaughts ploughed through the seas.

Once, aboard a destroyer as it knifed along the Maine coast, he asked the commander for permission to take the wheel. The commander turned pale, but he knew he could not say no to his boss. Franklin took the wheel and spun the destroyer around. The skipper grinned, his fears gone. Later he said, "From the moment he took the wheel, I knew he was a born sailor."

The Germans had promised President Wilson to stop sinking

American ships. But the Germans did not keep that promise. American ships carried food and guns to England. In March of 1917, a German sub blew up an American ship. "We have to go to war," Franklin told President Wilson, "since Germany already is at war with us!"

On the night of April 2, 1917, the President stood before the Congress. Franklin and Eleanor sat in the balcony of the hushed chamber. In a piercing voice, the President asked for a declaration of war. "The world," he told the Congress, "must be made safe for democracy!"

Near midnight, Franklin and Eleanor walked back to their Washington home. Their five children slept. Their fourth child, Franklin Delano Roosevelt, Jr., had been born in 1914. John Roosevelt, their fifth, had been born in 1916.

Franklin was now 35. Teddy had been about the same age when he sailed to Cuba and rode back a hero. The next morning Franklin got a telephone call from Teddy who shouted into the mouthpiece, "You must resign! You must get into uniform at once!"

Franklin smiled. Now his dream to be a navy officer could come true. And now he could be the war hero that Teddy had been, that third step in Teddy's rise to the highest office in the land.

8

"This Is What We Are Looking For!"

The potbellied, tousle-haired Josephus Daniels wore a soft grin. He walked into President Wilson's office carrying a request from Franklin.

That rascal Roosevelt, Daniels thought to himself. Daniels knew that Franklin often went behind his back to ask the President about something for the navy. Franklin told people that Daniels was too slow and stodgy to run the navy. Franklin said that he and his aide, the scowling Louis Howe, should run the navy. Daniels knew Franklin said this, but he forgave Franklin. He knew Franklin wanted to make a name for himself so that one day he could be President. When Franklin asked him to take his request to the President, Daniels said yes.

The President listened as Daniels told him what Franklin wanted: command of a ship as a navy officer. The President shook his head.

"Tell the young man to stay where he is," Wilson said to Daniels. "Neither you nor I nor Franklin Roosevelt has the right to select his place of service in winning the war."

Franklin winced when Daniels told him he would not attain a life-long dream.

"I am going to be a desk warrior," a dejected Franklin told Louis Howe. The wily Howe told Franklin he could gain fame even as a desk warrior.

Franklin and Howe crisscrossed the country on railroad trains to visit shipyards. Franklin spoke to workmen and urged them to

Franklin (far left) poses with celebrities during a drive to sell war bonds for the U.S. Treasury. Kneeling in front are silent-screen stars Marie Dressler and Charlie Chaplin. Directly behind them are Douglas Fairbanks, Sr., and Mary Pickford.

build warships fast to wipe out U-boats. Howe took labor union leaders aside. He knew that these new unions could tell hundreds of thousands of their loyal members how to vote in postwar elections. He told the leaders that Franklin stood for the working man.

At a shipyard near Boston, Franklin told a supervisor to turn over a ship that had just been built. The navy needed it right away. The supervisor said no. He said he could not give the ship to the navy until the navy paid for it. Franklin said the navy would pay as soon as it got the ship. The supervisor smiled and said no.

Franklin smiled back. A few days later a squad of Marines marched into the shipyard. They pointed their guns at the supervisor and told him to hand over the ship. The marines sailed out of the yard aboard the ship.

"That Franklin Roosevelt means business," the supervisor said with a rueful grin. His name was Joe Kennedy. He had a baby named John Fitzgerald.

Those U-boats were always on Franklin's mind. They sank ships faster than the British could build them. Within a year, feared the British, they would not own enough ships to supply their island with what they needed to win the war: food for their people, arms for their troops.

U-boats sneaked into the English Channel. They lurked outside of harbors and picked off ships as they streamed into ports. Franklin had an idea: could a wall be built to block the German subs from slipping into the Channel?

Not possible, said British admirals. They agreed that a wall of mines might be strung across the north doorway to the Channel. When a sub touched a mine, the mine would explode and destroy the sub. The trouble was, at least 400,000 mines were needed for a wall wide enough and deep enough to block the Channel. The British and Americans did not have that many mines.

Navy officers called Franklin "a great trial-and-error guy." They said, "He'll try anything new. If it doesn't work, he'll cover up his mistake by trying something else new—and usually he finds something that works."

One day Franklin was sitting in his office. His door was always wide open to anyone who had an idea. A civilian walked in, carrying a bag. From the bag he took out an object that looked like a bowling ball. Long copper wires fluttered from the ball like strands of hair. The man, inventor Ralph Browne, told Franklin that when a sub touched one of those hairy wires, his "Browne Submerged Gun" fired a torpedo to sink the sub.

Franklin's eyes lit up behind his glasses. "This," he shouted, "is what we are looking for!"

Those hairy wires, he realized, could be attached to a mine instead of a gun. When a sub touched the wire, the mine would explode, and shock waves would sink the nearby sub. One mine, with hairy wires, could do the work of four mines.

"We don't need 400,000 mines!" Franklin told Daniels. "We can build a wall with only 100,000 mines."

Daniels shook his head. Even 100,000 mines would cost too much money. Franklin made an end run around his boss. He wrote a letter to Wilson and said of the wall, "It is vital to winning the war."

Wilson agreed. Within a year the navy had strung the wall across the Channel's mouth. The mines blew up as many as seven German subs in a few months. Franklin always liked to build up his part in winning the war. He knew that war heroes can become presidents. For years after the war he spun exaggerated stories to friends about how *his* invention (he forgot all about Browne) had won the war. In truth, the mines had helped—but only a little.

While Franklin fought subs, a harried Eleanor oversaw the education of her five children. She also had to give parties for navy officers or friends of Franklin's in the government. A relative suggested she get a social secretary to help her. Eleanor hired a family friend: a pretty 26-year-old Southern belle named Lucy Page. Lucy sent out party invitations. She worked with cooks and butlers on the entertaining and feeding of guests.

When "Babs and the five chicks" went to New York, Hyde Park or Campobello, Franklin stayed in Washington. Lucy also remained in Washington as a navy clerk. Often Franklin took Lucy to parties.

In Campobello during the summer of 1917, and in New York that fall, Eleanor read letters from Franklin telling of the fun he had at those parties with the pretty Lucy at his side. As Eleanor read those letters, a worried frown crept across her face.

In Washington, Franklin yearned to hear the guns of war. During the spring of 1918 he talked Daniels into sending him to France to inspect naval bases.

Landing in France, Franklin demanded to be taken to the front line. He heard the thunder of artillery. He insisted he and his party move closer.

He walked toward German trenches with a French patrol. He wore a helmet and gas mask. French troops encircled him and his aides. The soldiers gripped rifles and anxiously searched for machine gun nests.

"Hurry!" a French colonel shouted. "The German observation balloons have spotted us!"

Franklin ran to a clump of trees. He heard a shell's whine that grew louder and shriller. Then came a loud, dull boom.

He turned to see a puff of grey smoke plume upward near where he had stood seconds before. At last he had heard what soldiers call "a shot fired in anger." He had tasted the fear of oncoming death.

During the next three weeks he raced across France and Italy. After bouncing on shell-pocked roads from sunset to sunrise, his ears rang. He could not breathe. A navy doctor examined him and found he had pneumonia. A germ once more had struck him down.

Feverish and pale, Franklin sailed home. Sailors carried him off the ship on a stretcher when it docked in New York. An anxious Eleanor handed him a note. A smile crossed Franklin's sunken face as he read the note. It said, "We are very proud of you." The note was from Teddy Roosevelt.

In the only way possible for him as a desk warrior, Franklin had become the war hero he had dreamed of becoming as a boy.

While Franklin recovered in New York during the next few

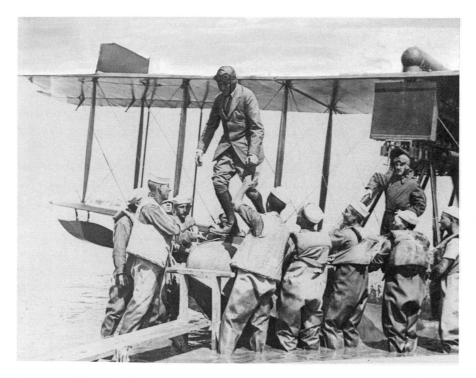

At a naval base in France, Franklin alights from a seaplane after a flight. The pilot (right) watches with fascination this daring young man willing to do anything he asked his officers and sailors to do.

weeks, Eleanor took charge of answering his mail. She opened one letter that had been sent to Franklin while he was overseas. It was a love note from Lucy Page. "My worst fears were confirmed," a stricken Eleanor later said.

Franklin and Eleanor talked of a divorce so he could marry Lucy. Franklin knew that a divorced man would never be elected President in his time. Women would soon be allowed to vote. Most would not vote for a man who had left his wife.

"If you want to be President, Franklin," Eleanor told him, according to a member of the family, "you'll have to take me with you."

Franklin promised never to see Lucy again. For the rest of her days, Eleanor could not bear to speak the name Lucy—even to a lifelong friend who had that name.

Eleanor stayed with Franklin as his wife. Never again, though, would they be close except when they shared ideas on politics and governing. She would care for him in sickness—more than she could ever have imagined in 1918—but not as an intimate. Eleanor began to realize she had to walk alone.

"The bottom dropped out of my own particular world," she said later. "I faced myself and my world honestly for the first time."

Eleanor turned her back on one world—the world of being the dutiful and almost slavelike wife—and began to look for doors to other worlds.

9

Buried Under a Landslide

"How old are you?" the delegate screamed.

"I'm thirty-eight!" Franklin shouted, his voice cutting through the din of the packed and steamy convention hall. "Why do you want to know?"

A day earlier the hundreds of delegates to the 1920 Democratic convention in San Francisco had picked Governor James Cox of Ohio to run for President. President Wilson had served two terms. Tired and sick (he would die a year later) he could not run again. Many Americans booed his name.

When the war ended in 1918 with Germany's defeat, soldiers came back from France and couldn't find jobs. Prices soared. Americans growled that Wilson had promised "a war to end all wars." He had tried to create a League of Nations where countries could debate with words instead of fighting with guns. U.S. senators had refused to allow the U.S. to sit in the League. It would be a failure—and so, thought many Americans at the time, was Wilson.

Franklin had left Wilson's cabinet at war's end. He walked the streets of Washington, forlorn, not knowing what to do next on a journey he had set for himself with the White House at its end. A Democratic leader stopped him one day and said, "The Roosevelt name is still famous. Many people admire you—people in politics, in labor, in big business. A lot of Democrats want you to run for vice president in 1920."

A family portrait taken about 1920. Anna is on the left, Elliot in the middle, James on the right. Franklin sits on his father's knee, baby John in his grandmother's lap. Eleanor holds a family picture album.

Franklin saw his goal suddenly loom so close he could almost touch it. The vice presidency had been the last stop on the route to the White House for Teddy.

That question about his age—screamed at him by the convention delegate! Standing now on the noisy convention floor, Franklin realized why the question had been asked. A person had to be at least 35 to be nominated.

"I am thirty-eight!" Franklin shouted.

"Leave the hall—I am going to nominate you!"

Franklin strode from the hall. By tradition, a candidate did not stay on the floor to hear himself exalted. Franklin's son, Jimmy, now 13, watched his tall, bronzed father and thought, as he said later: "He is the strongest, most physical father in the world."

Franklin waved a long cigarette holder at a friend as he went through a door. He smoked cigarettes—too many, Eleanor feared—and he inserted the cigarettes into a long holder. He used the holder to protect a sensitive lip. The holder usually tipped out of his mouth at a jaunty angle, a pose that radiated tremendous self-confidence and charm. That jaunty look, and the tossing back of his head, would become his trademarks. He seemed arrogant when he tossed back the head and looked down his nose—"but now," said a friend, "he smiled when he did it."

Earlier at the convention, Franklin stood on the stage and his vibrant voice had urged the nomination of Al Smith as President. Al, the governor of New York, had risen from the docks. He wore a derby, puffed a cigar, and he talked out of the side of his mouth with a "toity toid 'n' toid" accent. He seemed a true Progressive—a man of the people who called for more humane working conditions for factory workers, especially women and children.

But Democrats hissed when Franklin shouted for Al Smith to be nominated.

Al was a Catholic. Delegates muttered that a Catholic President would take orders from his religious leader, the Pope. Al lost the nomination to James Cox.

Cox didn't want Catholics and New Yorkers mad at him because he had beaten Al Smith. He thought Al's friend, Franklin, would attract easterners and Catholic votes.

"We want Roosevelt! We want Roosevelt!" Cox delegates shouted in the convention hall. Franklin beamed as he came into the hall to accept the nomination. He was running for the nation's second highest office just ten years after his entry into politics.

Franklin and Cox rode across the country on a special railroad train. They stood on stages in theatres and vaudeville houses. Only a few cities had radio stations. But when Franklin spoke into a radio microphone, listeners smiled standing next to their loudspeakers as they heard that voice vibrate like a gong as he began, "Maaa---ahhhh friennnnnndsssss . . ."

At night Franklin sat in his railroad car chatting with politicians. Or he played his favorite card game, poker, with newspaper pals. Eleanor often sat alone.

During the past few years she had visited war wounded in hospitals. Once she saw a dirty hallway where veterans sat in wheelchairs. She marched angrily into a Wilson aide's office. She demanded loudly that the hospital be cleaned. The next day the hospital gleamed.

Louis Howe began to sit with Eleanor on the train as it rumbled across the dark countryside. He talked to her of the day's happenings, for instance, how a certain mayor had asked that his cousin be named postmaster of a village. Howe explained why the job would go to the cousin. The mayor could get thousands of people to vote for Cox and Roosevelt.

Eleanor listened quietly, brown eyes intent. Politics, she had been taught as a girl, was a dark and ugly world. But now she asked Howe: if a politician like Cox would promise a job for votes, would a politician also help the hungry and homeless poor if that would also get him votes?

"Of course," Howe said. Politicians would do almost anything for votes.

Eleanor thought for hours about what Howe told her. She talked to other politicians. "Before long," she said, "I was finding myself

Governor Cox and his running mate come to the White House to talk to President Wilson during the summer of 1920. They were shocked to find the President disabled by a stroke and barely able to talk. Wilson's wife and a few close aides kept his condition a secret while they acted as the real president.

At Hyde Park in the summer of 1920, Franklin and Eleanor (far right) get the official word from party leaders that he is their choice to run for vice president. Cox, in the white suit, stands in the middle. On his right is Governor Al Smith, who would try four times to become the first Catholic President. After his last defeat, in 1932, he said, "I guess the country's not ready yet for a man to say the rosary in the White House."

discussing a wide range of subjects with other people in politics." One who listened to her closely was Franklin's friend, Governor Al Smith.

Franklin and Eleanor went back to Hyde Park to hear the election returns. Franklin was sure that the Republicans—Warren G. Harding for President and Calvin Coolidge for vice president—

would win. The nation was sick of eight Democratic years of war and bad times.

Franklin was right. But even he was shocked by the weight of the Republican landslide. The Republicans won six of every ten votes. It was the most lopsided presidential victory in a century.

Franklin grinned as he glanced at the returns. "Thank the Lord," he said to his newest aides, secretary Margaret (Missy) LeHand and press adviser Steve Early, "we are all comparatively youthful."

Franklin had earned $5,000 a year as a navy secretary. That was good pay at a time when few Americans earned more than $2,000 a year. But Franklin and Eleanor had ten servants, five children to educate, and they dressed, ate, traveled and lived like the other millionaire members of society's "400."

Franklin and Eleanor had inherited about a quarter of a million dollars. Interest from that money paid a small fraction of the bills. Sara, Franklin's mother, sent $5,000 checks for birthdays, $10,000 checks at Christmas. And when Franklin had no money to pay bills, Sara paid them. But Franklin and Eleanor wanted to pay their own way.

Franklin took a $25,000 a year job in New York as vice president of a banking company. He got business for the company by calling on friends he knew in the government. He worked there only in the mornings. In the afternoons he crossed Wall Street to work in a law firm owned by himself and a friend. That brought in another $25,000 a year. $50,000, plus interest, was enough to pay their bills.

Franklin put Louis Howe on the law firm's payroll. Louis had one job: to keep Franklin's name in the newspapers so that voters didn't forget the Roosevelt name.

Franklin worked ten hours a day. At nights he made speeches at charity banquets—speeches arranged by Louis to keep him in the spotlight. On weekends he and his five children hiked through the woods near Hyde Park. "Everything Franklin does," a friend said, "he does at full speed ahead."

This is the last photo of Franklin walking unaided. He leads a parade of Boy Scout leaders and their troops at a camp on the Hudson. That evening he boarded a boat to go to Campobello. His lean, taut face shows his fatigue.

In the summer of 1921, Eleanor and the children left for Campobello. Franklin labored in Wall Street's baking hot offices. Franklin's secretary Missy LeHand wrote to Eleanor that he seemed exhausted.

He decided to go to Campobello—his first vacation since before the war. But the morning of the day he had to leave, he trekked north to a Boy Scout camp along the Hudson. He marched in a parade. His face looked drawn and taut.

That evening he stepped aboard a friend's yacht to sail up the New England coast. Storm and fog swirled off that coast. And at the journey's end, a grinning devil named polio awaited him.

Franklin's courage and ambition were now to be tested—while millions watched.

—

10

"The Happy Warrior"

Franklin gripped the wheel of the yacht. He had steered the boat all night long through a storm that tossed the yacht as though it were a pencil. The boat rose and plunged while Franklin peered into a thick fog. The boat's skipper stood at his side. He had given the wheel to Franklin, who knew these waters. Franklin's friends crowded the deck, holding lines and wondering where they were being tossed—toward Campobello or out to open sea and disaster.

A smile broke over Franklin's weary face. He shouted, "Welshpool Harbor, dead ahead!" His friends let out a cheer.

Franklin bounded off the yacht. He stayed up much of the next night with his friends to watch how the islanders fished. The next afternoon he and his friends sailed across the Bay of Fundy for an afternoon of fishing. Once, baiting a hook, Franklin slipped into the water. He popped up laughing. But later he said, "I never felt anything as cold as that water"—water he had swum in happily all his life.

The next day he sailed offshore with his five children. They spotted a brushfire on an island. He and the children—Anna, at 15 the oldest, Johnny at 5 the youngest—raced into searing heat and choking smoke. They put out the fire.

Later they jogged two miles and dived into the ocean for an hour of swimming. That evening Franklin's body ached. He said he had a bad cold. He went to bed early.

51

The next morning he awoke and swung his legs off the bed to get up. The left leg collapsed. He rested a few minutes, then tried to rise again. Both legs gave way. Sitting on the floor, he stared with a puzzled frown at his legs.

Then the pain struck.

It came in waves during the next few weeks as paralyzed muscles shrank. He had been stricken by infantile paralysis, the dreaded polio virus that killed and paralyzed thousands each year. The pain cut so viciously that a flapping bedsheet made Franklin wince.

Men carried him on a stretcher to a boat and then onto a train to New York. After weeks of treating him, doctors wrote on his records: "No improvement."

He would get well soon, he told people. Josephus Daniels came to visit him. Daniels walked toward the bed. Franklin reared up from his pillow and threw a punch to Daniels's midsection. Franklin grinned and shouted, "You thought you were going to see an invalid. But I can knock you out in any bout."

When visitors left, he shouted after them, "Goodbye now. I've got to run." He roared with laughter.

Doctors fitted his paralyzed, withered legs with heavy iron braces. Those "metal muscles" helped him to walk. He swung one heavy foot, then the other. One hand gripped a cane, the other hand the arm of a strong companion.

"Doctors say I'll soon throw away the braces and canes," he cheerfully told people. No doctor ever told him that. But he seemed to believe it—most of the time.

He usually showed Eleanor, his children and his friends only a smiling face. In his bed he chinned himself on iron bars above his head to strengthen his upper body. At Hyde Park he crawled down the driveway, sweating, growling to himself, "I have got to reach the road." Those crawls, he hoped, would build up the withered muscles of his legs. When he got to the end of the driveway, panting, he stopped before turning to crawl back. He waved gaily to neighbors passing by.

But no cripple could expect to walk into the White House. Frank-

His withered legs dangling from the side of a boat, Franklin looks over a fish caught by him and his friends off Florida. In the first two years after polio paralyzed him, he went frequently to Florida to swim in the hope that swimming would bring back strength to his legs.

lin's son Elliot later recalled one incident of "the dark moods," as Elliot called them. One morning Franklin shouted in an empty room, "Has God abandoned me?"

He admitted to one fear—that a sudden fire at night might trap him in bed. Unable to get out of bed without aid, he feared he might be burned to death.

In 1924, three years after that painful sunrise at Campobello, he heard that a polio victim had begun to walk after swimming in the mineral-water pools of a resort at the mountain village of Warm Springs in Georgia. The "resort" was actually a clump of ramshackle buildings. The warm water in the pools came from hot underground caverns.

His servants lowered Franklin by his arms into one of the mineral-water pools. He could stand in the warm, soothing, buoyant water. It was the first time he had stood without aid in three years. He grinned as he looked up at the servants, exclaiming, "I don't think I will ever get out." He wrote to his mother, "These waters will make me as good as new, you just wait."

A month later an Atlanta newspaper reported that the famous Franklin Roosevelt had come to nearby Warm Springs and "was swimming his way back to health and strength."

Polio victims read the story. Hundreds wrote to Franklin at Warm Springs. Could they come?

Franklin wanted to help them. But where would they all stay? Some of the buildings seemed ready to fall down. But Franklin, always willing to try anything once, had an idea.

He had a new law partner in New York, the energetic and shrewd D. Basil O'Connor. Franklin called O'Connor and said he wanted to buy the broken down resort. He would fix up the buildings where people could stay while they tried to swim their way back to health.

O'Connor said he was crazy. So did Eleanor and Sara. "You'll go bankrupt," they protested. "You can't make money out of a place for sick people."

But Franklin insisted. He paid almost $200,000 for the old buildings and the pools. Polio victims came by car and train to Warm

"Dr. Roosevelt" stands in the center of a pool at Warm Springs. Other members of his "Polio Gang" stand or swim in the buoyant mineral water. The water helped the polio victims to feel better. None were able to walk normally again.

Springs. They swam in the pools. Franklin fluttered his legs with them. Each morning, as he was wheeled to the side of the pool, he shouted, "Hello, members of the Polio Gang. Here is Dr. Roosevelt. Now remember: You've got to know you are going to improve!"

Franklin shuttled between Warm Springs and his Manhattan banking and law offices. His children seldom saw him. Anna had gone to college. The high-spirited, playful Anna was his favorite. Jimmy, his oldest boy, was the "good boy" of the family, hard-working, eager to be a famous political figure like his father. Elliot was "the bad boy." He hated to read books and brought home Cs on report cards. Franklin and John, the two youngest, played pranks on other kids. Once they rode a pony too fast. Wheezing, it had to be taken to a veterinarian. As punishment, Eleanor said they could not ride the pony for a year.

A day later she and Franklin saw the boys leading a new pony to pasture. Sara, who lived with them at Hyde Park, fawned over the children. She had heard of the punishment. She gave the boys another pony.

"They're spoiled by her," Eleanor said. Franklin shrugged. "What am I going to do?" he said, "I know they are spoiled by her. So was I."

As the children left home to live at school—all the boys went to Groton and Harvard—Eleanor had time for outside work. She joined the League for Women Voters. She became friendly with women from the New York State Democratic Party. She admired Al Smith and spoke about him to meetings of women voters.

Louis Howe sat in the rear of halls, listening to her. Her voice was shrill. She giggled nervously. After listening to one of her speeches, Howe took her aside and said, "Where did you get that terrible giggle? Don't be nervous. Have something you want to say, say it, and sit down."

Eleanor would always have a shrill voice, but she lost the giggle.

She remembered what Howe had told her—politicians would do almost anything to get votes. She knew that Al Smith still yearned to be President. She told the New York State Governor that nonCatholic women would vote for him if he passed more laws to make life easier for women and children laboring in factories and sweatshops. By 1924 New York led the nation in laws protecting women and children.

When Franklin came to New York, he and Louis Howe often talked late into the night. By now Calvin Coolidge sat in the White House as President. Warren Harding had died in office. Prosperity boomed across America. Salaries soared, farm prices jumped, and the stock market spiraled higher and higher.

This was the Jazz Age, the Golden Twenties. Americans laughed and danced at the most dazzling, richest, giddiest party the world had ever seen. Everyone, it seemed, could own a car, a radio, a house. If you picked the right stocks, ones that leaped from a dollar

to $100 a share in a few months—and that happened all the time—
you could even waltz through this party as a millionaire.

"The Republicans are getting all the credit for this boom," Howe
told Franklin. "They will win the presidency in 1924, 1928 and
probably in 1932. But the bottom will fall out of this boom. There
will be a bust, a depression. There always is. Then people will elect
a Democrat to the White House to pull them out of the hole."

Franklin and Howe agreed. Franklin should keep on trying to
walk again. Howe, meanwhile, would stream letters to Democrats
across the nation to remind them that the Roosevelt name could
win the Presidency in 1936.

In the summer of 1924, the Democrats gathered in New York's
Madison Square Garden to pick a candidate to oppose Cal Coolidge.
Al Smith asked Franklin to stand before the convention and nom-
inate him for President.

Eleanor and Howe looked at each other anxiously. Franklin had
not stood on a stage in three years. Few people saw him except
when he sat behind a desk. How would he look to Democrats as
he tried to walk awkwardly across a stage to speak? Suppose—and
this had happened—his cane slipped. He'd crash to the floor, and
millions would hear the crash on their radios.

Franklin decided to speak. In his office he marked out the space
he would have to walk. For weeks he struggled to swing himself
across that space.

At a Garden filled to the rafters with 15,000 people, men hoisted
him onto the back of the stage. The delegates could not see how
helpless he was. Holding his cane and Jimmy's arm, he moved
awkwardly to the front of the platform.

Spotlights picked out the handsome face with the glittering pince-
nez glasses. Flashbulbs popped like fireflies in the night. He walked
awkwardly across the stage, holding Jimmy's arm and leaning on
the cane. He lunged at the rostrum and gripped it. He hoped his
weight would not topple it over and send him crashing to the floor.

Then he looked up at the jammed balconies. He tossed back his
head, flashed the huge smile, and waved.

Wet-eyed men and women began to applaud. The applause swelled into a loud and long roar—Franklin was back!

Still holding tight to the rostrum which shielded those crippled legs, Franklin began to speak. He said that Al Smith stood next to the farmer and the laborer as a true Progressive. Al Smith, he said, fought for the small man against big business. Then he gave Al Smith a name that would stick with the feisty Al a lifetime—"The Happy Warrior."

Delegates rose and cheered. Franklin waved. That night, propped on a pillow in his bedroom, he grinned as he read papers headlining his "Happy Warrior" speech. Once more he was famous across the country. "I made it! I made it!" Franklin shouted to a friend. Another "Happy Warrior" had come back to the political battlefield.

11

"Please Pray for Me, Jimmy"

The phone rang, shrilling loudly against the stone walls of the cottage in Warm Springs. Franklin rolled his wheelchair to the phone. He picked it up and heard the scratchy voice of Louis Howe, calling from New York.

"Smith wants you to run for governor, Frank. You have got to say no."

"You're right," Franklin said quickly. If Al Smith called, he told Howe, he would refuse to run.

Franklin put down the phone. He guessed that Smith would call any minute. He thought about the four years since his Happy Warrior speech for Al Smith in 1924.

The Democrats had snubbed Smith again, picking John Davis, a Southern lawyer. The Republicans and Calvin Coolidge swamped Davis.

Franklin was still a banker and lawyer in Manhattan, a polio patient and "doctor" in Warm Springs. His law and banking firms pulled in hundreds of thousands of dollars as money flowed freely on Wall Street. Franklin poured much of the money into the Warm Springs treatment center for polio victims. By 1928 it had become the nation's No. 1 treatment center for polio.

Howe and Franklin still believed that the Roaring Twenties would roar into the 1930s—and then crash. In 1936, they believed, a Democrat could promise to pull Americans out of the wreckage and be elected President.

This is believed to be the only photo ever taken of Franklin in a wheel-chair. It was not published. The dog on his lap is probably Fala. Franklin is trying to jolly a tearful girl embarassed by all the attention. A polio victim with one leg in a brace, she was a poster girl for a March of Dimes campaign. That was the first of the fund-raising drives that have since collected billions to defeat cancer, heart disease and other killers.

Franklin and a small friend fish at a creek near Warm Springs. Few photos showing the thinness of his legs were published during his lifetime. Boys and girls born during the 1930s did not realize that their President could not walk.

In 1928 the Republicans nominated Herbert Hoover, a California engineer, to run for President. Cal Coolidge, his two terms finished, retired. Hoover had endeared himself to America and the world with a plan that saved millions of Europeans from starvation after the World War. He was a moon-faced man who seldom smiled.

The Democrats finally picked New York Governor Al Smith as their nominee. Al could not run for both governor and president. He wanted a sure-fire vote-getter to run for governor.

"I have got to carry my own state to beat Hoover," Al Smith told Howe in the summer of 1928. A ticket of Al Smith for President and Franklin Roosevelt for governor, he said, would guarantee that New York dropped into the Democratic pocket.

Howe and Franklin were certain that Smith would lose. Any Republican, they thought, would win in these boom times. If Franklin ran for governor, he would be buried under all those Republican votes. And if Franklin couldn't win an election in his own state, how could he convince Democrats in 1936 that he could win across the country for a presidency?

The phone rang again in the Warm Springs cottage. Franklin picked up the phone. He heard Al Smith's growl: "I need you to run for governor."

Franklin reminded his old friend: he still couldn't walk. In two or three years, he said, his legs would be strong enough to campaign. Besides, Franklin said, he wanted to give all of his time to making Warm Springs a shining place of hope for his Polio Gang.

Desperate, Smith had to look for another candidate. He could find no sure winner. He called Eleanor to his headquarters the night before the Democrats had to pick a candidate for governor.

"Frank won't return our phone calls to him in Warm Springs," he told Eleanor. "Frank will take a call from you. Please call him. When he answers, just hand the phone to me."

Eleanor hesitated. She didn't want to trick her husband. But she admired Al Smith. She dialed the number in Warm Springs and told the operator to put her through to Franklin.

"Hello, Babs," Franklin said. He sat in a phone booth in a drug store where he had been hiding from Smith's calls.

"Hello," Eleanor said. She handed the phone to Smith and quickly left the room.

Smith told Franklin he had to run to help the party. Franklin had to think fast. If he said he would not run, how could he expect support from Smith and New York Democrats when he asked them to help him become President in 1936?

"If these fellows will nominate you tomorrow," Smith persisted, "will you accept?"

"I don't know."

Smith got the message one politician had just flashed to another— *Franklin had not refused*! "All right," Smith shouted. "I won't ask any more questions."

The next morning the Democrats nominated Franklin. Smith and Franklin knew he had to accept. If he didn't, Democrats would label him a traitor.

A furious Howe called Franklin and began to scold him. Franklin cut him off. "I've got to run for governor," he said. "There's no sense in all of us getting sick about it."

Franklin shakes hands with his two political wizards, Louis Howe on his right, and Jim Farley, on his left. Howe was too sick, his lungs damaged by cigarettes, to be close to Roosevelt as President. Farley became the No. 1 political adviser. In 1940 he broke with Franklin, arguing that a third term was bad for the party and the nation.

History had begun to beckon Franklin Roosevelt to step into its glare.

Franklin decided to show New York voters that he had vigor and strength even if he couldn't walk alone. He rode in the back of an open car, just as he had driven in a roadster in his first campaign 18 years earlier. Aides hoisted him onto the back of the car to speak to groups in villages and at crossroads. Just as he had done 18 years earlier, he began each speech with that toast-warm greeting, "Miii-ahhh frriendsssss . . ."

His lungs ruined by cigarettes, the wheezing Louis Howe stayed in Manhattan to oversee the campaign. A balding former minor league first baseman, James Farley, rode around the state with Franklin. Farley had grown up in a small Hudson River town. At 17, he was elected to a town office before he was old enough to vote. He knew every Democratic leader and most every precinct captain in the state. He never forgot a first name. He slapped town leaders on the back, men he hadn't seen in a year, and said, "How have you been, Billy? And how is your wife Betty?"

The flattered leaders promised Jim Farley to get out every possible vote for Franklin.

Hoover walloped Al Smith in Smith's own state—and most everywhere else. Hoover won 40 of 48 states, the most lopsided presidential victory ever up to then.

But Franklin nudged ahead of the Republican nominee for governor to win by a razor-thin margin—25,001 votes of more than 4 million ballots. Crowed Franklin, "I cast that one vote." From Virginia, Democratic leader Harry Byrd wired Franklin, "You are the hope of the Democratic party."

The crash came sooner than Howe and Franklin had expected. In October of 1929, the stock market streaked downward like a child on a greased slide. It kept on dropping in 1930 and 1931. Americans gulped as billions of dollars in paper profits vanished.

Lots of Americans owed money for the radios, refrigerators, cars and homes they had bought on credit during the Roaring Twenties. They couldn't pay those debts by selling stocks. Stocks were nearly worthless. People could only afford to buy the bare essentials.

Factories had to shut down. Long lines of jobless men and women stretched for miles. Hungry people waited for a small bowl of cold soup.

In Chicago, a restaurant put out a can of garbage. Some 50 men, women and children fought each other with fists and teeth to grab half-eaten pieces of smelly, discarded food.

Franklin summoned to Albany what would soon be called his "Brain Trust." They were college professors, labor experts, money wizards. He asked them for ideas to help the jobless and the poor.

"Let's try everything and anything," Franklin told the Brain Trusters. "If one thing doesn't work, we'll try something else. Above all, *try something!*"

He asked for new laws to aid the victims of what was being called the Great Depression. He told state legislators: "The duty of the state toward the citizen is the duty of the servant to his master . . . caring for those of its citizens who need help . . ."

Franklin boosted the income taxes of the rich. He gave $20 million for jobs and food to the homeless and poor. Money flowed out of Albany to pay wages for the new jobs created by the state. The money fed hungry children. Other states watched what Franklin was doing with envy.

In Washington, President Hoover seemed to do nothing. He told Congress and Americans not to worry—"prosperity was just around the corner." As Americans turned the corner of another new year, they heard the crying of their hungry, frightened children.

In 1931 and early 1932, Jim Farley raced across the country. He told Democrats that Franklin could win back the White House. He asked delegates to the 1932 convention to vote for Franklin.

The convention opened in a steamy Chicago arena in July of 1932. Al Smith still yearned to be president. So did a crusty Texas rancher, John (Cactus Jack) Garner, who was the Speaker of the U.S. House of Representatives.

Sitting next to a radio in Albany, Franklin and Eleanor listened as the delgates voted on the first ballot. A candidate needed 770 votes to win the nomination. On the first ballot Franklin got 666, Smith 201, Garner 90.

The delegates went on voting through the night, ballot by ballot. At dawn Franklin still led, but he was shy of the 770 votes. The weary delegates streamed out of the indoor stadium into the baking heat and slouched off to their hotel rooms to sleep.

Jim Farley stopped Sam Rayburn, a bald and stumpy Texas congressman. He was a friend of Garner's. "If Texas votes for Roosevelt," Farley whispered to Rayburn, "Frank will pick Garner as vice president."

Rayburn shrugged. At his hotel he phoned Garner in Washington. Garner didn't want to be vice president. As Speaker of the House, he gripped more power than anyone except the president. Vice presidents, he knew, were ignored. "The vice presidency," he said, "isn't worth a pitcher of warm spit."

Garner told Rayburn he would call him back. A newspaperman came into Garner's office. He told Cactus Jack that the powerful publisher, William Randolph Hearst, Jr., a Garner supporter, wanted Garner to quit the race. Hearst feared that the weary delegates might compromise and choose a weak candidate, a candidate Hoover could beat.

Garner agreed. He called Rayburn and told him to switch all the Texas votes to Franklin. Those votes would put Roosevelt over 770.

That evening the delegates gathered for another ballot. Suddenly, a rumor swept the arena: Texas had switched to Roosevelt! No delegate wanted a future President mad at him.

Chicago's mayor, Tony Cermak, grabbed a microphone. He shouted that Illinois switched its votes to Franklin. Other state leaders jumped up to join the stampede. Minutes later the convention had picked Franklin as its nominee for president. Bands struck up "Happy Days Are Here Again," Franklin's theme song.

Franklin flew to Chicago. In his ringing voice, he told the delegates: "I pledge you, I pledge myself, to a new deal for the American people."

A new deal! The three words stuck in people's imaginations. A new deal! A new start! Franklin Roosevelt's administration, not yet born, had a name that would last its lifetime and beyond.

Franklin easily beat Hoover, carrying 42 of the 48 states, the most in any presidential election up to then. Democrats captured the majority of seats in the House of Representatives and the Senate. Franklin knew he would get the votes from Congress to pass the laws he wanted.

On election night Franklin watched the returns at a Manhattan hotel. That night his son Jimmy helped him to bed.

"You know, Jimmy," the President-elect said. "All my life I have been afraid of only one thing—fire. Tonight I think I am afraid of something else."

"Afraid of what?"

"I am afraid that I may not have the strength to do this job. Please pray for me, Jimmy."

Jimmy said he would. He switched out the light and carefully closed the door. Meanwhile, a thousand miles away in Chicago, a madman had bought a pistol, slipped it into his pocket and promised himself that he would kill this President Roosevelt.

12

A Christian, a Democrat —and a Mechanic

He slid his hand into his coat pocket and gripped the pistol as he watched the president-elect. Franklin Roosevelt sat on the back seat of the open car. A small group of people ringed the car. They had just watched Franklin leave a fishing boat. The humid Florida air hung over this park in Miami on a February night in 1933. People stood on tiptoe to see the man who would be sworn in as president a month from now.

Giuseppe Zangara's stomach ached. Presidents made his stomach hurt, he told himself. If he killed this president, maybe his stomach would stop hurting.

Franklin waved as people applauded his short speech. Chicago mayor Tony Cermak came up to the car and leaned forward to talk to Franklin.

Zangara walked swiftly toward the car. He stood only 20 feet from Franklin. He whipped out the gun and pulled the trigger. The gun roared in his hand.

People screamed. Bullets banged loudly against the side of the car. Franklin whirled. He saw secret service men rush at Zangara and topple him to the ground.

Cermak staggered. Blood splotched his shirtfront. A cop yelled, "Get Roosevelt out of here!"

"I'm all right! I'm all right!" Franklin shouted. "Get Tony over here and drive to the hospital."

Cops carried the bloody Cermak to the car. They placed him in the back seat next to Franklin. "You'll be all right, Tony," Franklin said, cradling the mayor in his arms.

"Thank God it wasn't you, Mr. President," Cermak said as the car raced through the dark streets.

Cermak died the next day. Zangara was executed for the murder. A secret service man told a friend, "The President was calm even later, when you'd think the shock might have hit him. That night I looked into his room several times. Each time Mr. Roosevelt was fast asleep."

An icy wind whipped the flags that fluttered over Pennsylvania Avenue. A large crowd of almost 10,000 people stood facing the white stone building. They had just watched Franklin sworn in as President.

Franklin faced a row of radio microphones. The mikes would carry his inaugural speech to a nation that seemed frozen in ice.

Banks had closed their doors. The banks had loaned money in the boom 1920s to people who now had no jobs. The people couldn't pay back the loans. Banks didn't have the cash to give to people who had left their life's savings in the bank.

At this moment, in millions of homes, fathers and mothers put their hands into empty pockets or purses and wondered: how will I feed my children tonight?

In his stately voice, Franklin told a listening America:

"This great nation will endure as it has endured. It will revive and it will prosper."

Then he gave strength to the frightened with words that would always be remembered by those who lived through the harrowing years of the Depression: "The only thing we have to fear is fear itself."

To every problem, he was saying, there are answers.

He came forward with answers during the next three months of his New Deal—what became famous as his "First Hundred Days." "The Roosevelt Whirlwind," thankful congressmen called it. Frank-

Franklin is sworn in as the nation's 32nd President by Supreme Court Chief Justice Charles Evans Hughes. Franklin was the first President whose mother could vote for him. Women had not been allowed to vote before 1920.

lin bulleted demands at the Congress and said, "Turn these into laws that will pull fallen people to their feet."

Jobs! He had to put people to work. They would earn wages. With money jingling in their pockets, they could buy food. Farmers would get higher prices for their crops. The farmers could buy new tractors. To make those tractors, factories would have to hire workers. That would mean more money in more pockets, more buying, more production, more workers—and, most important, fewer poor people.

In those hundred days and the months that followed, Franklin signed laws to create New Deal agencies that gave people jobs. The Civilian Conservation Corps (CCC) hired more than a quarter of a million young men to work in forests and national parks. The Works Progress Administration (WPA) hired eight million men and women to build roads, bridges, tunnels and airports. The National Youth Administration (NYA) hired millions of high school and college students to work in libraries and schools.

The President signs bills into laws, assisted by his secretary Grace Tully. On the wall behind him are framed portraits collected by a boy and man who had a lifelong love of the sea and its ships. One of the 1930s laws signed by Franklin gave cheap electricity to farmers. The most famous of these projects was the Tennessee Valley Authority (TVA).

Another new agency, the Agricultural Adjustment Administration (AAA), paid farmers to plough under plentiful vegetables. Prices shot up for those harder-to-find vegetables. Farmers earned the money to pay off loans, buy tractors, and keep their farms.

Some people—the old, the sick, the widows with small children—could not work. Franklin set up the Federal Emergency Relief Administration. It sent "home relief" checks to those who could not work. In its first two hours, the home relief agency poured out more than five million dollars.

Franklin brought his Brain Trust from Albany to Washington. There were economics professors like Rexford Tugwell and law geniuses like Felix Frankfurter. Labor experts like Frances Perkins came, and Franklin made her the first woman member of the Cabinet in U.S. history. Eleanor applauded when Franklin announced his choice of Perkins. Eleanor had become one of America's leading feminists. Frances Perkins often banged her fist on a table and demanded better working conditions for factory workers—and got them.

Other Brain Trusters included financial wizard Henry Morgenthau, who became Secretary of the Treasury, and the tough boss of national parks, Secretary of the Interior Harold Ickes. Harry Hopkins, a scarecrow-thin, rumpled Midwesterner, who was Chief of the Emergency Relief Administration, dug into the treasury's vaults to ship out millions of dollars in home relief checks.

Franklin's political advisers, Jim Farley and Louis Howe, came to Washington. Farley was made Postmaster General, and he kept Franklin's stamp collection filled. His main job, though, was to look for ways to reelect Franklin in 1936.

"You dumb Dutchman!"

Louis Howe often shouted these words at Franklin when he thought the President had made a mistake. Franklin laughed, but he listened. Franklin's advisers gulped. No one else dared to talk that way to the most powerful man in the nation. But Franklin had never forgotten how Howe had made the nation think he stood tall

In this photo, taken by a friend and not published in his lifetime, Franklin's withered legs can be seen clearly. He holds Fala. Behind him is a roadster that was equipped with hand controls so he could drive it. He liked to race the car across the Hyde Park estate, often scaring his passengers while he roared with laughter.

and strong during the 1920s while he labored in the shadows at Warm Springs to try to walk again.

Many Americans, both Democrats and Republicans, began to worry that Congress had given Franklin and the New Deal too much power. The critics said that Franklin had become a Fascist dictator like Germany's ruthless leader, Adolf Hitler, or a Communist like Russia's brutal ruler, Josef Stalin.

At a birthday party for the President that raised money to fight polio, the President is surrounded by "handmaidens" dressed like himself in wreaths and Roman togas. On his right are Sara and Eleanor. The Roman costumes were the idea of press aide Steve Early to twit Republicans who had started to compare Franklin to a Roman dictator.

A reporter once asked Franklin, "Mr. President, are you a Communist?"

"No."

"Are you a capitalist?"

"No."

"Are you a socialist?"

"No."

The reporter asked what he did believe in.

Franklin shrugged. "I am a Christian and a Democrat, that's all," Franklin said.

Actually he was a mechanic tinkering with a car that would not start. The mechanic tries a new battery, new spark plugs, a new carburetor, until the engine coughs and roars to life.

Franklin came to a car that had rolled to a stop. His New Deal gave it new parts: the WPA, the AAA, home relief.

Previous American presidents would have left the car alone. "It ran too fast during the boom time and something busted," they would have said. "Let it rest, and it will start running again."

The car's passengers, meanwhile, would die of hunger or sickness before the car rolled.

Franklin said, "We are the servants of the passengers, so we must be the mechanics who give the car what it needs to run again."

All the presidents who followed him, Democrats like Harry Truman and Republicans like Ronald Reagan, agreed with Franklin that government had to help those—the sick, the old—who could not help themselves.

From 1933 to 1939 America climbed upward from the valley of the Great Depression toward prosperity. In 1933 Americans earned about 42 billion dollars. By 1934 they were pocketing almost 50 billion. They took in 76 billion in 1937 and by 1939, the Depression ended, they took in more than twice what they earned when Franklin took office—about 90 billion dollars.

Never since has America slid into a depression. The reason, many people think, is that the American car can not stall and stop. The government stands ready to pep up the engine with "fuel"—jobs.

Franklin had to stay in Washington during those hectic first four years in office to prod the Congress into passing New Deal laws. He asked Eleanor to be his "legs." She traveled all over the country to see that the New Deal really was helping people.

Once she visited a poor family in West Virginia. As she was leaving the bare-walled, cold house, she saw a little boy gripping to his chest a white pet rabbit. He stared at her, eyes wide with fright. His older sister saw Eleanor look at the boy.

The sister smiled and said, "He thinks he's going to keep that rabbit. But it's going to be cooked for supper tonight."

The boy burst into tears and ran out of the house, still holding tight to the rabbit. Eleanor saw many such heart-sinking sights as she visited families struck down by the Depression.

Eleanor seemed willing to go anyplace to see what Americans needed. A magazine, *The New Yorker*, published a cartoon showing two miners deep underground. One was saying to the other, "Good gosh, here comes Mrs. Roosevelt!" A few weeks later Eleanor actually did drop into a West Virginia mine.

Eleanor once left the White House early to visit a prison in Baltimore. Later that day Franklin asked Eleanor's secretary where his wife was.

"In prison," the secretary said.

"I am not surprised," Franklin said, "but what for?"

13

The President a Little Dog Knew

Franklin sat at his desk facing Frances Perkins. Outside the windows of the Oval Office they could see roses blooming in the garden on this spring morning in 1935. Franklin, who loved to talk, liked to toss ideas at his Brain Trusters.

"Why shouldn't we have a cradle-to-grave insurance system?" he said to his Secretary of Labor. "Once a child is born, he or she would become part of the social security system. When the person starts to work, he pays part of his wages for insurance. His employer would also pay something.

"If the worker loses his job, he gets weekly benefit checks—his insurance. If he is sick, he gets insurance payments. And when he is over 60, he can retire and live off his insurance checks from social security for the rest of his life."

Frances Perkins agreed. Later that year the president signed the Social Security Law. A year later Eleanor got a letter from the widow of a coal miner killed in an accident.

I am going to get social security benefits of nearly sixty five dollars a month," the widow wrote. "I pay fifteen dollars a month rent. I can raise vegetables and chickens. With the social security money, I will get along well. In the past the company might have given me a small check and other miners would raise a collection. But this social security money I can count on. Thank your husband for social security.

Franklin later called social security the cornerstone of his New Deal. The tinkerer had become the inventor. He had found a way to put money into Americans' pockets even when they didn't have a job because of bad times, sickness or old age.

And as long as people had money to spend, they could buy. Factories would stay open. Farmers would sell their crops. There could never be another Great Depression.

Franklin usually awoke about eight. He grumped and growled until he had his first cup of coffee and a cigarette. "Then," an aide once said, "the clouds went away from his face and the sun came out."

Servants lifted him from his bed to a wheelchair. He shaved sitting in the wheelchair. A valet helped him to dress. He wheeled the president into his office and helped him into a swivel chair. Franklin sat in that chair behind his desk for the rest of his workday.

Piles of reports, as many as a thousand, sat high on his desk waiting to be read. By late that night he had read them all and dictated comments and replies for each of the thousand to his secretaries, Missy LeHand and Grace Tully. If a report ran more than two pages, he gave it back to Missy or Grace and said, "Tell them to boil this down to a single page and I'll read it!"

He talked for hours on the phone. The phone was his "legs," his way of finding out what was going on in Washington and around the nation. And what he was told—by writers, professors, politicians, all kinds of experts—he did not forget.

One morning an aide handed him a sheet with a long list of people to be promoted. He scanned the list. He checked off four names and said, "These four are not loyal to the New Deal."

"But we have been told they are," the aide protested. He wondered why Franklin thought they weren't loyal.

"That's what I hear. See if I am right."

The aide investigated. Later the aide said, "Of the four he had checked off, all four turned out to be what he had said—not to be trusted."

Visitors filed into his office all day. Each wanted something from the President. He listened for a few minutes. Then he began to tell a story. Often it was the same story the visitor had heard during his or her last visit. But while Franklin told his drawn-out story, he was making up his mind whether to say yes, no, or maybe to his visitor's requests.

When a visitor talked, Franklin had a nervous habit of saying, "yes, yes." It was his way of hurrying the visitor along so Franklin could start to speak. Some visitors thought the "yes" meant "OK" to their request. Later, when a visitor was told by a presidential aide that his request had been turned down, he accused Franklin of lying. One congressman stormed at Franklin, "The next time I get a yes from you, it will have to be in writing."

Indeed, he hated to say "no." So he rarely did. And he hated to bring bad news to someone. He never fired an assistant who wasn't doing his job. He would just stop seeing the person, hoping he or she would resign—and they usually did.

He lunched at his desk, usually with a visitor. His favorite lunch was boiled trout. He had become heavy in his midsection, his barrel chest the width of heavyweight boxer Jack Dempsey's. Doctors said he should lose weight, so he skipped desserts.

He talked even as he ate. When a visitor wanted to pop a request at Franklin, he waited until Franklin dug a fork into his lunch. Then, as Franklin began to chew on his food—and couldn't talk—the visitor had half a minute to ask for what he wanted.

At 5:30 he left the office to swim or float in a White House pool built for him. He napped for half an hour, then wheeled himself into his study for what he called "the children's hour." He mixed cocktails for himself, his family and guests.

One guest was the King of England. Before the King came to the study, Sara told Franklin, "The King will have tea instead of a cocktail."

The King arrived. "Would you like tea or a cocktail?" Franklin asked. "My mother does not approve of a cocktail."

"My mother doesn't either," said the King as he reached for a cocktail.

Dinner was nearly always the plain, nonspicy kind of food that

Eleanor liked. Franklin liked French and Italian-flavored food but
said nothing. Guests often said, "When you are invited to the White
House for dinner, it's wise to eat somewhere else first."

After dinner Franklin liked to watch a movie. He enjoyed news-
reels, Mickey Mouse cartoons and any film with actress Myrna
Loy. He liked to irritate his mother by making loud remarks about
the charms of actresses on the screen.

Other evenings he bent over his stamp collection. Or he sat in
the living room and played games with a little black Scotty named
Fala. A friend gave the dog to Franklin, who had loved dogs since
he was a child. During the day Fala flopped on the floor near
Franklin's wheelchair. At night the dog slept at the foot of his bed.

The President usually went to bed about midnight. A servant
lifted the President from the wheelchair into his bed. He liked to
read mystery novels, finishing a dozen in a week, before he nodded
off to sleep. Once Eleanor gave him a new novel, *Gone With the
Wind*. The next morning he told her he had finished it.

"How could you?" she asked. The novel ran more than 700
pages.

Franklin rattled off the names of the characters in the book and
told her the story. Eleanor often said that she knew no one who
could read as fast as Franklin and remember so much—"like a
sponge," she said.

Franklin fled from Washington in the summer to the place he
had loved since he was a child—the sea. He sailed off the coast on
the presidential yacht *Potomac* or on a navy warship. He sat on
the deck chatting with men like Harry Hopkins while he gripped
a fishing pole and tried to catch a marlin or other deep-sea fish.

Each January 30th, Franklin's birthday, celebrities like radio
comedian Bob Hope and the movie star Carole Lombard flocked
to the White House for the President's Birthday Ball. Other balls
were held across the nation. People paid to come to those parties.
The money went to Warm Springs so that more polio victims could
enjoy the soothing pools.

Basil O'Connor had set up the Infantile Paralysis Foundation to

On a vacation from the presidency, Franklin sits at the helm of a sailship with his son Jimmy. By the end of Franklin's first term, the rich people who had known him at Groton and Harvard called him what a previous generation had called cousin Teddy—"a traitor to his class."

oversee those balls. The Foundation began a yearly fund-raising campaign called the March of Dimes. Dimes mounted into millions of dollars that went to scientists trying to find a polio vaccine.

That vaccine was found some ten years after Franklin's death. By the late 1950s children were being innoculated with the vaccine. Never again in America would a man, woman or child have to live in the braces that imprisoned Franklin for the last 30 years of his life.

"What is the President really like?"

Reporters put that question to Brain Trusters like Harry Hopkins and Henry Morgenthau. Frances Perkins summed up most of their answers: "He is the most complicated human being I have ever known."

One day Secretary of the Interior Harold Ickes said to him, "You are one of the most difficult men to work with that I have ever seen."

"Because I get too hard at times?" Franklin asked, smiling.

"No, you never get too hard. But you won't talk frankly with people who are loyal to you. You keep your cards close to your belly."

Franklin had to be a smart poker player. He had to get a lot of New Deal laws passed, and he had to make New Deal agencies work hard to help poor Americans.

Franklin knew that if the men and women working for him didn't know what he was thinking, they worried. They would wonder: Does the President think I am doing a good job or a bad job? As a result, they worked harder to make the New Deal succeed.

Once Franklin told Henry Morgenthau, "Never let your left hand know what your right hand is doing."

"Which am I?" asked Morgenthau, "the left or right hand?"

"The right hand," Franklin said, laughing. "But I keep my left hand under the table."

"That," Morgenthau later said, "was the real Franklin Roosevelt and how he worked."

Eleanor and Franklin's five children had begun to marry. By 1946, most had children. Each New Year's Eve, the family gathered at the White House to welcome the new year.

Franklin told the grandchildren his favorite jokes. He liked to tell the jokes that Roosevelt haters were telling each other, for instance:

A man always bought his newspaper each morning from the same newsboy. Each day the man scanned the front page, then threw

Most of the Roosevelt family gathers for a Christmas at the White House. On the left are Eleanor and Sara. Franklin is shaking the hand of Franklin Delano Roosevelt III, who sits on his mother's knee, her husband Franklin D., Jr., behind her. Behind Franklin is his son John. On John's left is John Boettiger, the husband of Anna. She and the other grandchildren watch one of their own drawing all the attention away from the President of the United States.

the paper away. One day the boy asked, "Why do you read only page one?"

The man said, "I'm only interested in the death notices."

"But they're on the back pages," the boy said.

"Boy," the man said, "the one I'm interested in will be on page one!"

Franklin threw back his head and roared, "I love it! I love it!"

As the clock inched close to midnight, Franklin handed out glasses of eggnog. At midnight, as bells chimed in the new year, Franklin raised his glass and shouted, "To the United States of America!"

Eleanor, the children and the grandchildren rose, raised their glasses and chorused together: "To the United States of America!"

14

A Third Term, a War —and a Secret Bomb

"I see one-third of a nation ill-housed, ill-clad and ill-nourished."

Rain spattered on the pages of his speech as Franklin spoke on a wet March day in 1937. Minutes earlier, a Supreme Court justice had sworn in Franklin for his second term as President. The previous November he had swamped the Republican candidate, Kansas governor Alfred Landon, by winning 46 of the 48 states—the widest margin of victory up to then in U.S. history.

The New Deal had pulled many Americans out of the pit of the Depression, Franklin told the listening nation. But one-third of the nation's 140 million, he said, still lived in misery.

"It is not in despair that I paint you this picture," Franklin said. "I paint it for you in hope"—hope that soon every American would eat decent food, wear warm clothes and live under a roof that didn't leak.

Franklin had fired off a barrage of demands to Congress: a minimum-wage law that forced employers to pay at least 40 cents an hour to their workers and a National Recovery Act (NRA) to funnel more money to the poor and jobless. Congress rubber stamped its approval on almost everything that Franklin wanted. Most congressmen and senators were Democrats who had been elected by clinging to Franklin's coattails.

But the U.S. Supreme Court—"those nine old men," Franklin angrily called its justices—struck down 11 of 16 New Deal laws. The laws, said the Court, violated the U.S. Constitution.

The Court often voted 5 to 4 against Franklin. Franklin wanted to appoint more judges who would favor the New Deal so he could win those close votes. He sent a bill to Congress to allow him to add three new justices.

Many Americans were shocked. Franklin, they said, was trying to pack the Court with judges friendly to him. Even most Democrats opposed what they called the "packing of the Court."

To get his Court packing bill made into law, Franklin told Vice President "Cactus" Jack Garner to round up votes. Cactus Jack came back to the White House and told Franklin in his slow Texas drawl, "You're beat, you haven't got the votes."

Franklin laughed. But inside he seethed with anger. He'd show the Congress who was boss. In the 1938 elections he would tour the nation and tell voters not to vote for those congressmen who had stopped his Court packing bill.

Franklin boarded a train that rolled south to Texas. There he spoke for a young congressman who had campaigned for the Court bill—Lyndon B. Johnson. But in Colorado in the West, Georgia in the South, Nebraska in the North and New York in the East, he asked that the voters throw out of Congress the men he wanted purged.

"Are you going to let an outsider tell you how to vote?" the senators and congressmen asked their voters.

"No, sir," most voters said. Nearly all of the "purged" candidates were not purged—they won. "What do you think of the President's purge?" a reporter asked Jim Farley. "It's a bust," Farley said glumly.

Louis Howe had died in 1936. Only Howe had been able to tell Franklin that he was wrong. Harry Hopkins became Franklin's closest adviser, but he served more as a messenger. He took Franklin's orders and passed them down to aides below him.

The packing of the Court and the purge of the Congress were unsuccessful. "If Louis Howe had been alive," Eleanor often said, "Franklin would never have made those two mistakes."

This picture, later autographed by Franklin to one of his favorite congressmen, was taken shortly after Lyndon B. Johnson was elected to the House of Representatives in 1937. In the middle is Texas Governor James Allred. Franklin, coming ashore after a vacation cruise, met Johnson on a Galveston dock. Days later, in Washington, he told aides that one day Johnson could be President.

Some Americans, who had greeted Franklin as a lifesaving knight on horseback in 1933, now spoke scornfully of him. He had become too bossy, they said. Others spoke bitingly of what they called "the disgraceful behavior" of his children.

By 1938 all five had been married at least once. All five would divorce and remarry. Highway police stopped Franklin and John, the youngest, and gave them tickets for speeding. Gossip columnists wrote of the Roosevelt boys drinking, dancing and even brawling in nightclubs.

Franklin conceded that his five onetime "chicks" were no angels. He knew he had not given them enough of his time and advice when they were growing up. "When one of my children wanted to see me," he once said, "they had to make an appointment through my secretary. That wasn't the right way. If I had been less occupied, a lot of things might have been different."

Joe Kennedy, the World War I shipyard foreman, had become a millionaire. He bought stocks as they soared during the 1920s, then sold them for cash in 1929. He had piles of cash as the Great Depression dawned—cash he could loan to people to make himself richer. He handed out cash to Democrats, including Franklin, who needed money to run for office. Now Joe Kennedy wanted his reward. Standing in Franklin's office on a spring day in 1938, he told the president: Name me the U.S. ambassador to Great Britain.

"Joe," the president said, "would you mind taking down your pants?"

The wiry Kennedy stared aghast at the president. But when Franklin asked again, he undid his suspenders and dropped his pants. He stood in front of the president in his undershorts.

"Joe, just look at your legs," Franklin said. "You're the most bowlegged man I have ever seen. Don't you know that the ambassador has to go through a ceremony in which he wears knee britches? Can you imagine how you will look? You're just not right for the job, Joe."

Kennedy told Franklin he could get permission from the British to wear long pants at the ceremony.

Holding back his laughter—he knew he would give Kennedy the job—Franklin said that Kennedy had two weeks to get permission.

Two weeks later, permission in hand, Kennedy was appointed ambassador to Great Britain. Franklin told friends how he had talked the millionaire into taking down his pants. Franklin laughed so hard he had to wipe tears from his eyes. "I love it! I love it!" he shouted.

Kennedy arrived in England with his son, John F. Kennedy, a Harvard student. They saw Europe biting its nails as Germany's bold Adolf Hitler grabbed territory. In 1938 he had marched into Austria. Now he wanted to seize Czechoslovakia. British leaders tried to appease him.

Franklin knew that America could not stop Hitler. The U.S. Army had only 118,000 soldiers, fewer than Mexico. Its double-winged planes, its lumbering tanks and its rusty guns dated back to the World War. With Americans starving, Franklin had not wanted to spend money on guns. But now he began to ask more money from Congress for tanks, planes and warships.

> *"I'd give my head if I could learn,*
> *Who'll be my boss next year."*

Franklin grinned as he read the lines of poetry given to him by his slim secretary, Grace Tully. She gave it to Franklin on his 58th birthday—January 30th, 1940. Like millions of Americans, including Eleanor, Grace wondered if Franklin would try to become the first President to win a third term. Cousin Teddy had tried—and lost. When reporters asked Franklin if he would run, he laughed but would not answer yes or no.

Franklin told Eleanor, Jim Farley and Harry Hopkins that he wanted to retire to Hyde Park. He had erected a stone building next to the mansion where his mother, now in her 80s, still lived. The new building housed the Franklin D. Roosevelt Library. He had set up an office in the library. From there he hoped to write articles and books and perhaps his life's story. At times he looked exhausted with dark half-moon smudges under his eyes. His hands shook. Doctors worried about the four packs of cigarettes he smoked each day. But after a trip to Warm Springs or a two-week sea voyage, he came back to Washington looking refreshed and waded into piles of work.

Cigarette holder tipped at a sharp angle from his mouth, Franklin leaned forward to hear the voice as it broke through the radio static from 3000 miles away.

"We shall defend our island whatever the cost may be," the British voice said. "We shall fight on the beaches, on the landing grounds, in the fields, in the streets and in the hills. We shall never surrender."

Speaking on this June day in 1940 from London was British Prime Minister Winston Churchill. Britain stood alone, an island surrounded. Nine months earlier, in September of 1939, France and England had declared war on Hitler when his troops marched into Poland. Hitler conquered Poland, then turned around and charged into France. In six weeks his tanks and dive-bombers swept over France. The British army escaped across the Channel to England. It came ashore bloodied and rag-tag; British tanks and guns were strewn on French beaches. The invincible Nazi army stood on the Channel shore, ready to spring at the throat of England. German subs sneaked under the Atlantic to cut off the island from the rest of the world.

Like most Americans, Franklin prayed that England could bounce off the ropes to defeat Hitler. "We'll be next after England," some Americans said. "Hitler is out to conquer the world."

Franklin sent warships to Britain. American destroyers convoyed ships carrying food and supplies to the British. Franklin, meanwhile, signed a law drafting men into the armed forces. He told Americans that the nation must prepare to defend itself. Defense, to other Americans, meant preparing for a war they thought the nation could not dodge.

Thousands of Jews had fled to America to escape Hitler's death camps. One, a scientist, asked for permission to speak to Franklin.

"What do you know of nuclear fission?" the scientist asked Franklin.

"Not much," Franklin said. Anything technical, from economics to engineering, confused him.

The scientist told Franklin that nuclear fission could create a bomb that would blow up entire cities with one blast. The scientist said that Hitler's scientists were working to split the atom and build such a bomb.

"Pa!" Franklin shouted, calling for his military aide, General Emmett (Pa) Watson. "This is something important," he told Pa. "Get your people working on it." Within weeks American scientists began work on the supersecret Manhattan Project.

In the summer of 1940 the Democrats assembled in Chicago. The delegates asked each other the same question: "Will he run for a third term?"

Just before the convention, Franklin told Jim Farley that he would not run. But Franklin knew that if he chose not to run, the delegates would probably pick Jim Farley, Cactus Jack Garner or Secretary of State Cordell Hull. All three, he knew, disliked many New Deal laws. The laws were too tough on big business, they said, too nice to labor unions. If Farley, Hull or Garner became President, Franklin knew, they would tear down the New Deal structure he had built.

Then there was the war. Franklin believed that neither Farley, Hull nor Garner knew how to build up an army and navy to fight a war.

Franklin decided to run for a third term. He knew Cactus Jack didn't want to be a New Dealer's vice president. Franklin chose as his vice presidential running mate a fervent New Dealer, Secretary of Agriculture Henry Wallace, whom many Democrats disliked. They said he was a foolish daydreamer.

The delegates happily picked Franklin over Farley and Garner. But they howled when asked to pick Wallace. If he became President, said many politicians, how could they trust a dreamer to do what he promised? The delegates angrily talked about rebelling and choosing someone else.

In Washington, Franklin wrote a note saying that if the delegates did not pick Wallace, he would not run.

Eleanor flew to Chicago. No longer the shy, giggly speaker, she stood in the middle of an arena packed with 15,000 delegates and spectators. Millions listened on radio. She said that this was no time

Campaigning during the summer of 1940 for a third term, Franklin shows his hand-picked vice presidential choice, Henry A. Wallace. In 1948 Wallace ran for President as a third-party candidate. He lost to the Democrats' Harry Truman.

for Democrats to bicker. "This is a time," she said in a firm voice, "when it is the United States we fight for."

The delegates stood and cheered. They nominated Wallace. Harry Hopkins phoned Eleanor and said, "You saved the day for Wallace."

She laughed. "You young fellows have got to learn a thing or two about politics."

The education of Eleanor Roosevelt, politician and leader, was completed.

The Republicans nominated a tousle-haired industrialist, Wendell Willkie. As the campaign came nearer election day, Franklin was told that he might lose because American women feared he, the Wilson Democrat, would do what Wilson had done—send their sons and husbands to Europe to die.

Franklin wrote a speech promising not to send American soldiers into "any foreign war." Hopkins suggested he insert the phrase, "except in case of attack."

"No," Franklin said, "because if we're attacked it's no longer a foreign war."

That night American men and women cheered when he said, "I have said this before and before, but I will say it again and again, your boys are not going to be sent into a foreign war."

He would later wish he had listened to Hopkins.

15

"The Japanese are Attacking . . ."

"Well, I'm going to take some time off, Eleanor."

Eleanor nodded as she and Franklin sat together over breakfast in the White House on an August day in 1941. Franklin had defeated Willkie easily to do what cousin Teddy had failed to do—win a third term.

"Where are you going?"

"Oh, just a cruise on the Potomac off Cape Cod for some fishing."

Eleanor caught the glint in Franklin's eyes and was not fooled. She knew he was about to do what he always loved to do—spring a surprise.

The Potomac cruised the Cape Cod canal. Thousands of vacationers lined the banks to wave at Franklin. He waved back, the familiar cigarette holder tipped at the usual cocky angle. A dark blue navy cape covered his broad shoulders.

One night the Potomac veered out to sea. It met a navy cruiser, the *Augusta*.

The Potomac raced back to Cape Cod. The next morning the crowds again saw the familiar figure on deck, waving.

Franklin, meanwhile, roared with laughter aboard the *Augusta*. The secret service had planted a man who looked like him on the Potomac. No German spy could know where Franklin was going and the very important person he was meeting.

A British battleship ploughed through the Atlantic swells, dodging German subs. It carried Britain's leader, Winston Churchill. In

Franklin waves to the crowd as he rides with Eleanor to his third inaugural early in 1941. The smudges under his eyes were among the first
signs of a tiring President. By 1942, Eleanor was speaking out in the
White House to demand equal rights for blacks. Franklin told her he
could not speak out for those rights. "A leader," he told her, "can't get
too far ahead of his followers or else they will wander off to follow
someone else." He did not believe that white America of the 1940s would
have supported him in asking equal rights for blacks. In the 1950s
Eleanor became one of the leaders of the civil rights movement in the
U.S. and a fighter for human rights in the United Nations. She died in
1962.

a bay off Newfoundland, Franklin and the ruddy-faced, portly Churchill met. Churchill told Franklin that the Japanese, Hitler's ally, would soon strike at Southeast Asia to grab oil, rubber and other raw materials for its war factories. The Japanese, he said, would also strike at the U.S. owned Philippines. Churchill asked: Should the United States declare war on Japan before Japan struck?

No, Franklin said. Neither the United States people nor its armed forces were ready for war. But he promised that if the Japanese attacked, America would declare war against both Japan and Germany.

Churchill invited Franklin to join him on the British battleship for a Sunday morning religious service. Franklin agreed.

His aides frowned. They knew he could not be carried or wheeled aboard a foreign battleship. As the proud leader of a proud nation, he would have to step onto the ship.

Hundreds of British and American sailors stood stiffly on the battleship's deck. A British band stood ready to blare out the American national anthem the moment the President's foot touched the deck.

Franklin labored up the steep gangplank connecting the two ships. He gripped the gangplank's rails and swung his heavy braced legs. A hot morning sun glared down. Streams of sweat trickled down his face. He kept a grin fixed on his face as he moved slowly, chest heaving as he swung one leg, then the other.

On the battleship's deck, the pudgy Churchill stood with narrowed, anxious eyes. Suppose the President slipped on the gangplank? He'd crash headfirst onto the ship's steel deck.

Hundreds of sailors and officers held their breaths, watching Franklin heave himself across the gangplank. Suddenly Franklin stopped.

So did the hearts of Churchill and hundreds of others. Could the President go no farther? Would British sailors have to carry him aboard?

Franklin smiled. He swung his left leg, then the right leg, and the right foot touched the deck.

Franklin steps aboard the British battleship HMS *Prince of Wales* off Newfoundland to meet the pudgy Churchill. He holds the arm of an Air Corps officer who had been ordered by his commander in chief to come to this historic meeting—his son Elliot. A marine officer got the same orders and also came, puzzling over why he had been ordered to report to a navy cruiser. There Jimmy Roosevelt learned why from his laughing father who dearly loved practical jokes.

"Oh, say can you see . . ." The music wafted across the blue sea. A thousand British and American men sang out the words *". . . by the dawn's early light . . ."* They saluted a brave nation and president.

The next day the two leaders signed what they called "The Atlantic Charter." The charter proclaimed that "people everywhere" had the right to four freedoms—freedom of speech, freedom to worship God, freedom from want, and freedom from fear.

Those Four Freedoms would soon become the battle cry of nations united against tyranny.

The cabinet gathered around a large table. Franklin wore a black band on the sleeve of his jacket. His mother had died a few days earlier. She was 87. Minutes after she died in the Hyde Park mansion, the biggest tree on the estate crashed to the ground: Witnesses said there had not been even the slightest breeze.

Franklin nodded to Frank Knox, the secretary of the navy, to speak. Knox told the Cabinet that on the previous day, December 4th, 1941, the Japanese fleet had been seen steaming out of its ports into the Pacific.

"Where is it headed?" Franklin asked.

"We don't know but probably south," Knox said.

At that moment, its radios silent, the Japanese fleet steamed east—toward Hawaii and the big U.S. naval base at Pearl Harbor.

On Sunday, December 7th, Franklin lunched at his desk with Harry Hopkins. The phone rang. The caller was Frank Knox. "The Japanese are attacking Pearl Harbor," Knox told the president.

"No!" Franklin said in a low voice. "No!"

16

The Long Voyage Home

Franklin wheeled the chair to the bathroom door. He knocked.

"Come in! Come in!"

Franklin pushed open the door. He saw the barrel-shaped body of Winston Churchill, pink and nude, standing in the bathtub.

Churchill waved his stubby arms and shouted, "Come in! The Prime Minister of Great Britain has nothing to conceal from the President of the United States!"

A few weeks earlier Franklin had spoken to the Congress. He called December 7th, 1941, "a day that will live in infamy." Congress declared war on Japan and its German ally, Hitler.

Churchill rushed to Washington. He feared that an angry Roosevelt would hurl all of his might into the Pacific to crush Japan. Churchill sat down at a table with Franklin and his silver-haired army chief of staff, General George C. Marshall.

"We must crush Hitler first," Churchill argued. Six months earlier, Hitler decided against an invasion of Britain. He plunged his armies into the vastness of Russia. The surprised Russians reeled backward against Hitler's armored fists. Russian leader Josef Stalin begged Britain—and now America—to invade France. Then Hitler would have to fight on two fronts: the British and Americans on the west, the Russians on the east.

Franklin nodded as Churchill asked that the allies destroy Germany first, Japan second. "Of course," he said.

Churchill's jaw dropped. "No argument?" he said, pulling his ever-present cigar from his mouth.

"No argument at all," Franklin said.

Soon there would be many arguments among the British, Russians and Americans. General Marshall wanted to plunge across the Channel to invade France—a short, straight-at-the jaw blow. Churchill wanted to invade North Africa, where his British armies now battled Hitler's Afrika Korps. From Africa, Churchill argued, the Allies could jump across the Mediterranean to sink their teeth into the Balkans—what he called "Hitler's soft underbelly."

Franklin stepped into the arguing. He made Marshall and the British agree to an overall war strategy:

Late in 1942 the Americans would invade North Africa. They would destroy the Afrika Korps. Then they would strike upward into Italy. But the biggest blow of all would come in 1944—that direct shot across France into Germany's heart.

General Marshall picked the man who would lead the invasion into North Africa and then France. His choice was a balding, square-faced general named Dwight David Eisenhower. His friends called him "Ike."

By late December of 1941, 26 nations had joined Britain, Russia and the United States in the war against Germany and its two allies, Japan and Italy. On New Year's Eve, Franklin and Churchill sat up late into the night at the White House trying to think of a name for those 29 allies.

The next morning Franklin again barged into the bathroom where Churchill sat in a suds-filled tub. "Winston," Franklin called from his wheelchair, "how about this name: the United Nations?"

Churchill reached for a cigar and said, "That ought to do it."

On that New Year's Day, 1942, the United Nations was born, pledged to fight for the four freedoms.

By late 1942 American factories turned out 125,000 planes a year, 75,000 tanks, millions of guns. The American army and navy swelled toward 12 million men and women. In the Pacific, General Douglas MacArthur began an island-hopping drive aimed at recapturing the Philippines and then leaping into the Japanese is-

The commander in chief salutes the flag with one hand over heart during a military review. On his right is General George C. Marshall, the army chief of staff. On his left is Admiral Ernest J. King, chief of the navy. Marshall was supposed to command the invasion of France, but Franklin wanted him at his side in Washington. The command went to General Eisenhower.

lands. In Africa, General Eisenhower's British and American troops sandwiched the Afrika Corps and destroyed it. In Russia, Stalin's troops began to push back Hitler's freezing legions.

Eleanor had crisscrossed the nation as Franklin's "legs" during the Depression. Now she circled the globe to report to him on how Americans were fighting World War II. In trips to the Pacific, she insisted on going to battlefields where men had died only weeks before. She trudged through mud to visit the wounded in hospitals.

An American marine lay dying. Doctors told Eleanor that battle shock had shattered the marine's will to live.

Eleanor leaned over the bed of the marine. "Son," she said, "I promise that when I get back home, I will visit your home myself to tell your mother how bravely you fought. But I will visit her only if you promise me you will try to get well."

The marine promised. Years later he and his mother visited Eleanor at Hyde Park to thank her.

Franklin's four sons wore uniforms. Jimmy, a marine colonel, led troops ashore on a Japanese-held island. A sniper shot a walkie-talkie out of his hand. Elliot flew Air Corps planes across Africa and Italy. John, a navy commander, won a bronze star for rescuing a sailor during an attack by German bombers. Franklin commanded a destroyer that guarded ships crossing the North Atlantic.

Roosevelt critics sneered that he had made his sons officers. A bitter Elliot wrote to Franklin, "Pop, sometimes I really hope that one of us gets killed so that maybe they'll stop picking on us."

The tall, blond Anna became Franklin's White House hostess during her mother's overseas trips. Anna had met Lucy Page Rutherfurd, the woman who had loved Franklin some 25 years earlier. Lucy, now a widow, lived near Washington with her daughter.

Anna liked Lucy and her daughter. She invited them to afternoon teas at the White House when her mother was away. She warned the servants not to tell her mother of Lucy's visits. Eleanor did not know that Franklin had broken his promise not to see Lucy.

In 1942 and 1943, Franklin and Churchill met at Hyde Park and at Casablanca in North Africa. By now American troops had driven into Italy. In the Pacific, navy battleships routed the Japanese fleet in the battles of the Coral Sea and Midway. MacArthur gathered his forces to pounce on the Philippines. British and American troops massed in Great Britain to leap across the Channel for the invasion of France in the spring of 1944.

Franklin knew that Britain, the United States and Russia would emerge from the war as the world's strongest powers. Franklin wanted Soviet Russia to be part of a United Nations that would keep the world at peace. He had to make Josef Stalin—"Uncle Joe," as he called him—a friend. A few weeks before Christmas of 1943, he flew halfway around the world to Iran. He met Churchill and Stalin in the ancient city of Teheran.

At Casablanca in 1943, Franklin makes a point during a conference with two of his generals. The four-star general is Dwight David Eisenhower, who became the Supreme Commander in the European Theatre, commanding British, Canadian, American and Free French troops. In 1952 he became president and he was reelected in 1956.

Just before a meeting with Stalin, Franklin pulled Churchill aside and whispered, "Winston, I hope you won't be sore at me for what I am going to do."

The roly-poly Churchill eyed Franklin suspiciously. Moments later Franklin wheeled himself to the elbow of the mustached, burly Soviet dictator. He began to whisper into Stalin's ear. In a whisper loud enough for everyone in the room to hear, Franklin said, "Winston is cranky this morning. He got up on the wrong side of bed."

For the first time, Franklin saw a smile crack Stalin's iron-hard face. During the next few minutes, Franklin said teasing things to

Stalin about Churchill: his plumpness, his smelly cigars, his British way of talking.

Churchill scowled, his face red. Stalin burst into laughter. "The ice was broken," Franklin said, "and we talked like men and brothers."

The three leaders talked about how the United Nations could keep future generations from wading into world war bloodbaths. Franklin left Teheran thinking Stalin trusted him.

He was wrong. Later Stalin told another Russian that Churchill was as harmless as a pickpocket who took only pennies. "But that Roosevelt," he said, "he dips his hands only for bigger coins."

Franklin flew home after the long trip, his face ashen. A cough racked his body. Doctors said his blood pressure had shot up, his heart had enlarged. They begged him to smoke less, eat less, work less. A navy doctor came to the White House each day to check his heart.

Franklin told his doctors, who suspected he had both cancer and heart disease, to say nothing to the press or the voters about his health. He had decided to seek a fourth term. As the 1944 elections came closer, the Republicans—who had nominated New York Governor Tom Dewey—published photos showing a slack-jawed, haggard Franklin. The Republicans said to the voters: "How can you trust a President who promised not to send your boys into a foreign war?"

Franklin showed a smiling, firm face to the voters. By the fall of 1944 Hitler's defeat seemed certain. Ike's troops had landed in France on June 6th. By late August American tanks raced toward the German border while Hitler cowered in a Berlin bunker. American and British bombers blew apart German cities.

Franklin knew American voters would want to reelect a winning President. But he also knew that party leaders could not work with the dreamy Henry Wallace if Wallace became President. Franklin had watched the rise to fame of another fervent New Dealer, Missouri Senator Harry Truman. He picked Truman to run with him as vice president. "Harry's a fine, honest man," he told Democratic party leaders. "He doesn't know much about foreign policy but he's

Aboard the cruiser *Baltimore*, which had taken him to Pearl Harbor in 1944, Franklin sits between his two Pacific chiefs: General Douglas MacArthur, on his right, and Admiral Chester Nimitz, on his left. In 1948 MacArthur made an attempt to become President, but the Republicans picked Tom Dewey, who lost to Truman. In the early 1950s MacArthur commanded U.N. troops in Korea. But he defied orders from Truman and was fired.

learning fast. I am going to turn things over to him after I make the peace."

Franklin knew he was sick, but he hid his weakening body from the voters. He visited a marine camp in California. Jimmy had arrived there to get ready for more battles in the Pacific.

Jimmy stared, shocked, when he saw his father. Franklin's suit seemed to hang like a curtain on his shrunken body. Suddenly, as Franklin chatted with Jimmy, the president's face turned milky white.

For the fourth time, Franklin rides to a Roosevelt inaugural, this time with his new vice president, Harry Truman, who sits between Franklin and a disappointed Henry Wallace. Typically, Franklin could not bear to give Wallace the bad news that he wasn't wanted. He sent Wallace to the convention thinking he would be picked. Then Franklin told party leaders that he wanted Truman, but Truman said no. When Franklin told Truman that he would tear apart the party if he refused, Truman finally said yes.

"Jimmy," he whispered, face clenched by pain. "I don't know if I can make it. I have horrible pains."

"I'll get a doctor."

"No!" Franklin asked Jimmy to help him stretch out on the floor. His body shook.

But an hour later he stood up, gripped Jimmy's arm and went out to wave for an hour to marching marines.

A month later Franklin won his fourth term, easily beating Dewey. On an icicle-cold day in January of 1945, he took the oath of office for the fourth time with Harry Truman at his side as the new vice president. A week later he slipped out of Washington and boarded

A grey-faced, haggard Franklin sits between Stalin and Churchill at Yalta. Arriving at Yalta, Churchill's face showed his shock when he saw Franklin. At times, he said later, Franklin's mind seemed to wander. Behind the leaders stand their advisers—England's Anthony Eden, America's Edward Stettinius, Russia's Vyacheslav Molotov. On Molotov's left is Averell Harriman, the U.S. wartime envoy to Moscow. Later he was the governor of New York.

a navy cruiser. It carried him on another long voyage half way around the world to Yalta, a Russian resort town on the Black Sea. There he met with Churchill and Stalin. He told Churchill that Britain and France would soon lose their grips on colonies in Southeast Asia, colonies such as Britain's India and France's Indo-China.

Winston growled angrily, "Never!" Franklin told him that the natives of those countries would rise up against the European colonists. Years later an Indo-China peasant leader, Ho Chi Minh, rose up against the French and later fought the Americans in Indo-China, renamed Vietnam.

At Yalta, Franklin and Churchill agreed to Stalin's demands for the carving up of conquered Germany and eastern Europe. Those agreements would later allow Stalin to drop what Churchill called "The Iron Curtain" over half of Europe and make Poland, Czechoslovakia, Hungary, and East Germany part of the Soviet empire.

Critics assailed Franklin for those Yalta deals. But others said, "What choice did he have?" The Soviets had captured half of Europe at a cost of millions of Russian lives. Only World War III, they argued, could force Stalin to give up what he had won.

Franklin rode home aboard the cruiser. On the long voyage back, one of his favorite aides, Emmett (Pa) Watson, died. Harry Hopkins had to be taken off the ship, deathly ill, and he and Franklin would never see each other again.

The ship ploughed westward across the tossing blue Atlantic. Franklin had always enjoyed these sea voyages. But now he sat alone, quiet, grey-faced.

Louis was gone, Pa was gone, Harry Hopkins was dying. Franklin gazed solemnly at a distant horizon.

17

His First Words
—and His Last

Jimmy walked into Franklin's study at Hyde Park. Through the windows they could see a January wind whip white curls onto the Hudson River. "I don't know when I will be seeing you again, pop," the marine lieutenant colonel said. "I'm off to the Pacific for the invasion of Japan."

His father smiled. He could not tell Jimmy what he knew. American scientists had just built an atom bomb. It could blow up Japan if Japan refused to surrender. "There will be no invasion of Japan," Franklin said. "You come back to me, son."

A few weeks later, in Washington, Frances Perkins came by the President's office to see the man she had known since he was an Albany legislator 35 years earlier. Her eyes widened when she saw the feeble Franklin. He was 63, but he looked nearer 80. His wasted body slouched in his wheelchair.

Franklin told Perkins he was leaving for Warm Springs to write a speech for the first meeting of the United Nations. It would be held in May in San Francisco. After that, Franklin said, "Eleanor and I will go to England for a state visit. I want to see the British people."

"I don't think you should go. The Germans could get—"

"The war will be over by May," he said. That day's newspapers told of allied armies streaking toward Berlin. Hitler would kill himself in a few weeks as Germany surrendered.

This is believed to be the last photo taken of Franklin. His cousin Daisy Suckley took it while Franklin pored over state papers hours before a stroke killed him. Even in this fuzzy photo, Franklin's body shows the signs of killing illness and exhaustion.

He rode by train to Warm Springs. Near noon on April 12th, he signed papers as an artist painted a portrait of him. The artist had been brought to Franklin's cottage by Lucy Page Rutherfurd, who had come to visit him along with two of his cousins, Laura Delano and Daisy Suckley. Eleanor laughingly called those adoring cousins "Franklin's lovely ladies-in-waiting." All his life he had delighted in being around women who adored him, beginning with his mother.

Franklin glanced at his watch. The time was a quarter to one. "We have 15 more minutes of work," he said. He signed a paper handed to him by an aide, then shouted to the laughing ladies, "Here's where I make a law!"

Franklin touched his hand to the back of his head. "I have a terrific pain in the back of my head," he said in a low voice.

He pitched forward in his wheelchair. Two servants ran into the room. They carried the unconscious President up to a bedroom. Three hours later his tortured breathing stopped. Doctors told a stunned and weeping nation that he had died of a stroke.

In Washington Eleanor got a call from Warm Springs that told her she was a widow. An aide said, "Mr. Truman is here."

The square-shouldered Truman walked into the room, nervously touching his steel-rimmed spectacles. He bent forward toward Eleanor and asked, "What can I do?"

"Tell us," Eleanor said to the new President, "what we can do."

On April 14th, 1945, in a somber Washington, a minister spoke at a simple funeral service. He told a quiet nation, listening on the radio, "They were his first words to us. I am sure he would wish them to be his last—'the only thing we have to fear is fear itself.'"

A few weeks later the United Nations met and began to lay the rules that have kept the world free of a global blood-bath for more than 40 years. Some four months later President Truman made the decision that death had spared Franklin from having to make. Truman ordered the dropping of the atom bomb that ended World War II and brought the nation to the dawn of an era of instant annihilation.

One of the things Franklin left behind was the memory of a beaming personality that made people who saw him feel that they had a friend and so there was nothing in the world to fear.

Franklin left a nation he had saved from fear itself. He left a world striving to attain the goals he had written during one of those sea voyages he loved—"freedom from fear, freedom to worship God, freedom of speech, freedom from want—for people everywhere."

Index

B
ROOSE
VELT

Devaney, John

Franklin Delano
Roosevelt,
President

$13.85

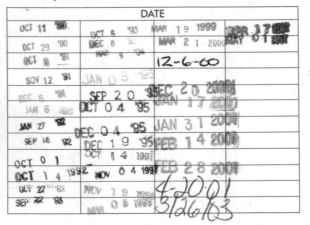

DATE			
OCT 11 '90	OCT 6 '93	MAR 19 1999	MAR 17
OCT 29 '90	DEC 8 '93	MAR 2 1 2000	MAY 01
OCT 9 '91	MAR 9 '94	12-6-00	
NOV 12 '91	JAN 03 '95		
DEC 6 '91	SEP 20 '95	DEC 2 0 2000	
JAN 6	OCT 04 '95	JAN 17 2000	
JAN 27 '92	DEC 04 '95	JAN 3 1 2000	
SEP 18 '92	DEC 19 '95	FEB 1 4 2000	
OCT 0 1	OCT 14 1997	FEB 28 2001	
OCT 1 4 1992	NOV 0 4 1997		
OCT 27 '92	NOV 1 9 1998	4-20-01	
SEP 22 '95	MAR 0 5 1999	3/26/03	